FLOYD CLYMER'S MOTORCYCLIST'S LIBRARY

The Book of the
PANTHER
(LIGHTWEIGHT MODELS)

A PRACTICAL AND COMPREHENSIVE GUIDE
FOR OWNERS OF 250 c.c. AND 350 c.c. O.H.V.
PANTHER MOTOR-CYCLES (COVERS MODELS
FROM 1932 TO 1958)

BY

W. C. HAYCRAFT, F.R.S.A.

SIXTH EDITION
1959

ANNOUNCEMENT

By special arrangement with the original publishers of this book, Sir Isaac Pitman & Son, Ltd., of London, England, we have secured the exclusive publishing rights for this book, as well as all others in THE MOTORCYCLIST'S LIBRARY.
Included in THE MOTORCYCLIST'S LIBRARY are complete instruction manuals covering the care and operation of respective motorcycles and engines; valuable data on speed tuning, and thrilling accounts of motorcycle race events. See listing of available titles elsewhere in this edition.
We consider it a privilege to be able to offer so many fine titles to our customers.

FLOYD CLYMER
Publisher of Books Pertaining to Automobiles and Motorcycles
2125 W. PICO ST.   LOS ANGELES 6, CALIF.

INTRODUCTION

Welcome to the world of digital publishing ~ the book you now hold in your hand, while unchanged from the original edition, was printed using the latest state of the art digital technology. The advent of print-on-demand has forever changed the publishing process, never has information been so accessible and it is our hope that this book serves your informational needs for years to come. If this is your first exposure to digital publishing, we hope that you are pleased with the results. Many more titles of interest to the classic automobile and motorcycle enthusiast, collector and restorer are available via our website at www.VelocePress.com. We hope that you find this title as interesting as we do.

NOTE FROM THE PUBLISHER

The information presented is true and complete to the best of our knowledge. All recommendations are made without any guarantees on the part of the author or the publisher, who also disclaim all liability incurred with the use of this information.

TRADEMARKS

We recognize that some words, model names and designations, for example, mentioned herein are the property of the trademark holder. We use them for identification purposes only. This is not an official publication.

INFORMATION ON THE USE OF THIS PUBLICATION

This manual is an invaluable resource for the classic motorcycle enthusiast and a "must have" for owners interested in performing their own maintenance. However, in today's information age we are constantly subject to changes in common practice, new technology, availability of improved materials and increased awareness of chemical toxicity. As such, it is advised that the user consult with an experienced professional prior to undertaking any procedure described herein. While every care has been taken to ensure correctness of information, it is obviously not possible to guarantee complete freedom from errors or omissions or to accept liability arising from such errors or omissions. Therefore, any individual that uses the information contained within, or elects to perform or participate in do-it-yourself repairs or modifications acknowledges that there is a risk factor involved and that the publisher or its associates cannot be held responsible for personal injury or property damage resulting from the use of the information or the outcome of such procedures.

WARNING!

One final word of advice, this publication is intended to be used as a reference guide, and when in doubt the reader should consult with a qualified technician.

INTRODUCTION

Welcome to the world of digital publishing ~ the book you now hold in your hand, while unchanged from the original edition, was printed using the latest state of the art digital technology. The advent of print-on-demand has forever changed the publishing process, never has information been so accessible and it is our hope that this book serves your informational needs for years to come. If this is your first exposure to digital publishing, we hope that you are pleased with the results. Many more titles of interest to the classic automobile and motorcycle enthusiast, collector and restorer are available via our website at www.VelocePress.com. We hope that you find this title as interesting as we do.

NOTE FROM THE PUBLISHER

The information presented is true and complete to the best of our knowledge. All recommendations are made without any guarantees on the part of the author or the publisher, who also disclaim all liability incurred with the use of this information.

TRADEMARKS

We recognize that some words, model names and designations, for example, mentioned herein are the property of the trademark holder. We use them for identification purposes only. This is not an official publication.

INFORMATION ON THE USE OF THIS PUBLICATION

This manual is an invaluable resource for the classic motorcycle enthusiast and a "must have" for owners interested in performing their own maintenance. However, in today's information age we are constantly subject to changes in common practice, new technology, availability of improved materials and increased awareness of chemical toxicity. As such, it is advised that the user consult with an experienced professional prior to undertaking any procedure described herein. While every care has been taken to ensure correctness of information, it is obviously not possible to guarantee complete freedom from errors or omissions or to accept liability arising from such errors or omissions. Therefore, any individual that uses the information contained within, or elects to perform or participate in do-it-yourself repairs or modifications acknowledges that there is a risk factor involved and that the publisher or its associates cannot be held responsible for personal injury or property damage resulting from the use of the information or the outcome of such procedures.

WARNING!

One final word of advice, this publication is intended to be used as a reference guide, and when in doubt the reader should consult with a qualified technician.

PREFACE

IN this handbook the author has made an earnest endeavour to provide in readable form just that information which all Panther owners need in order to obtain pleasurable riding free from trouble and unnecessary expense. The major portion has been devoted to such vital matters as lubrication, adjustments, and general overhaul, and early as well as recent models have been fully dealt with. So far as possible, descriptive matter has been avoided. Prospective buyers who want detailed specifications of current models have only to get in touch with Messrs. Phelon & Moore, Ltd., of Cleckheaton, or the nearest Panther dealers, when they will receive immediate attention.

Among Panther dealers in London may be mentioned: George Clarke (Motors), Ltd., (see advertisement); Jolly & Knott (see advertisement); E.S. Motors, Ltd., 325 High Road, Chiswick, W.4; Rowland Smith, Hampstead (Tube), N.W. 3; Rapid Motors, 269 Haydons Road, Wimbledon, S.W.19; Slocombes, 239-271 Neasden Lane, N.W.10; and L. Gillbanks, 283-5 New North Road, Islington, N.1.

Panther lightweight models are machines ideally suited for beginners, and during the compiling of this book the author has borne in mind that many of his readers may have spent only a few days in the saddle or perhaps may not have ridden at all. The present edition includes detailed instructions on the maintenance and overhaul of three groups of 248 c.c., 348 c.c. O.H.V. Panther lightweights—

(1) The 1932-9 P. & C. Red Panther Models 20, 30, 40.
(2) The 1938-48 P. & M. Panther Models 60, 70, 85.
(3) The 1949-58 P. & M. Panther Models 65, 75, and the 1950-3 Panther Model 65 de Luxe.

It does *not* cover the 600 c.c. Model 100 Panthers, two-stroke models, or the 250 c.c., 350 c.c. "Stroud" special competition models. The latter, however, are, except for competition

PREFACE

equipment, very similar to the corresponding standard models. The engines show no appreciable difference in design, but the 250 c.c. and 350 c.c. models both have magneto ignition fitted as standard.

Where instructions in this book are undated or specific models are not mentioned, the text applies to all P. & M. Panther lightweights and P. & C. Red Panthers from 1932 onwards.

All references to the 1949–53 250 c.c. Model 65 apply also to the 1950–3 Model 65 de Luxe, save in regard to the gearbox, which on the latter is a four-speed Burman.

The comprehensive maintenance instructions will, it is hoped, assist you to obtain maximum mileage, miles per gallon, miles per hour, and miles per pound. The author thanks Messrs. Phelon & Moore, Ltd., for helpful technical assistance, and for kindly permitting certain P. & M. illustrations to be reproduced, and George Clarke (Motors), Ltd., of Acton, for access to machines in their showrooms. Thanks are also tendered to the makers of various accessories for their helpful co-operation in connexion with this handbook.

W. C. H.

CONTENTS

CHAP.		PAGE
	Preface	
I.	ON THE ROAD	1
II.	TUNING THE CARBURETTOR	12
III.	CORRECT LUBRICATION	24
IV.	IN THE GARAGE	41
V.	CARE OF LIGHTING SYSTEM (1932–48)	106
VI.	CARE OF LIGHTING SYSTEM (1949 ON)	114
	Index	133

GEORGE CLARKE (MOTORS) LIMITED

THE LEADING PANTHER SPECIALISTS

FOR OVER 25 YEARS

FOR ALL YOUR PANTHER NEEDS

- IMMEDIATE DELIVERY ALL NEW MODELS — WE GIVE EXCEPTIONALLY HIGH EXCHANGE ALLOWANCE FOR USED PANTHER MOTOR CYCLES. WRITE FOR ALLOWANCE.
- HUGE SELECTION OF USED COMBINATIONS AND SOLOS AT BARGAIN PRICES.
- LARGEST STOCKISTS PANTHER SPARES IN UNITED KINGDOM, BY RETURN OR C.O.D. SPARES SERVICE.
- REPAIR SERVICE BY PANTHER EXPERTS — QUOTATION BY RETURN.

276/278 BRIXTON HILL, LONDON, S.W.2
TULSE HILL 3211/4 (6 lines)

275/9 HIGH STREET, ACTON, W.3
ACORN 6543 (2 lines)

OPEN WEEKDAYS 9 a.m. — 6 p.m.

CHAPTER I
ON THE ROAD

IT is presumed in this chapter that you are a novice and that your P. & M. Panther in all its glory of shining chromium and enamel is awaiting your commands in the garage or lock-up. It is also assumed that you have on your person a signed driving licence or provisional licence and a " certificate of insurance " and that you have fixed your registration licence in the circular holder provided on your machine, and an "L" plate at the front and rear if necessary. Keep the registration book safely at home.

Have you Ever Ridden a Pedal Cycle? Probably you have, and you will find this experience useful. If you have not, the author strongly advocates that you borrow a cycle for a few days as the sense of balance acquired gives immediate confidence on a motorcycle which actually is easier to balance on account of its greater weight and lower riding position. See also pages 81–2.

Getting the Machine Ready. Put the machine on the stand and if the tyres seem at all soft, pump them up to the correct pressures (see page 9). Next attend to fuel and oil replenishment. From a pump or with a can and funnel (having a gauze filter) pour about three gallons (250 c.c. models hold $2\frac{7}{8}$ gal.) of reliable-type petrol into the petrol tank and afterwards screw the filler cap firmly down. Then withdraw the oil sump dip-stick (combined with the filler cap on later models), and if the oil level is much below the *second* notch replenish with one of the reputable brands of oil mentioned on page 28. Be careful not to allow the oil level to rise above the top notch on 1932–58 models (see Fig. 13). On models prior to 1936 the filler orifice is situated on top of the timing case instead of on the near side of the sump, the oil gravitating to the sump. On all models fill to the dip-stick *top notch;* slightly below if over lubrication occurs.

In the case of pre-1936 Red Panthers the lubrication system has hand adjustment and full instructions will be found on page 29. Hand adjustment is not provided for 1936 onwards. The gearbox for the present can be overlooked as this is sent out filled with sufficient lubricant for about 1000 miles.

The Controls Explained. Before attempting to start up the engine you should get quite familiar with the purpose and working of the various controls which can conveniently be divided into

1

2 THE BOOK OF THE PANTHER (LIGHTWEIGHT)

two groups: (1) engine controls, (2) cycle controls. Most of them (all engine controls) are mounted conveniently on the handlebars and the Panther control layout is shown in Figs. 1 and 2. The engine controls are the throttle, air lever, ignition lever (where

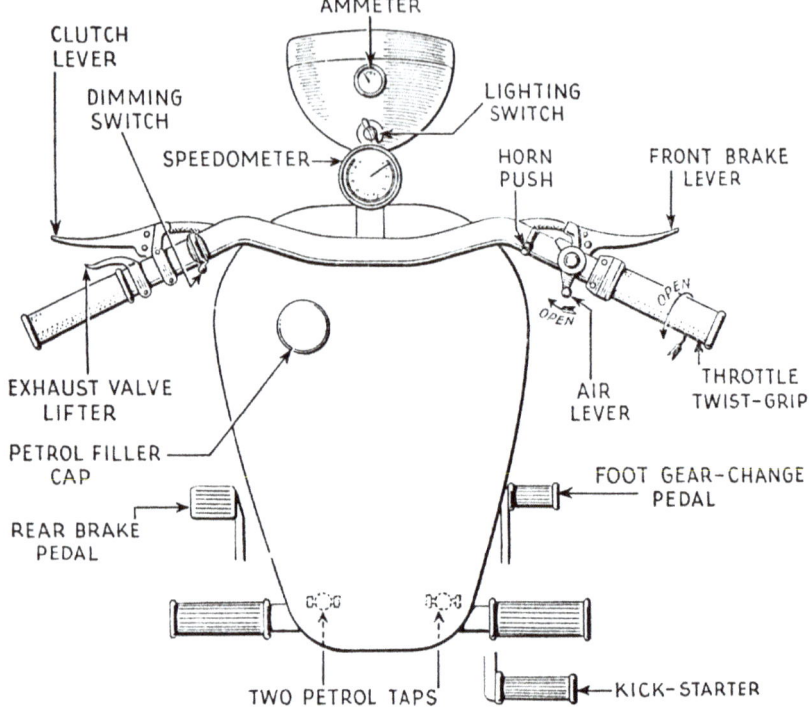

Fig. 1. The Panther Control Layout (1949 on)

The layout shown applies to Models 65, 75. On Model 65 (coil ignition), a warning lamp is incorporated in the centre of the ammeter and there is an ignition key in the centre of the lighting switch. 1949–54 models have no ignition lever, the spark being controlled by an automatic ignition advance mechanism. An ignition lever is fitted to the 1955-8 Models 65 and 75 (see also pages 3, 88, 121)

fitted) and exhaust-valve lifter. The cycle controls are the gear lever, the clutch, and the brakes.

The Throttle. The right-hand side of the handlebars terminates in a twist-grip which constitutes the all-important throttle control by means of which (as may be understood by perusing the next chapter) the volume of mixture supplied to the engine is increased or decreased according to whether the twist-grip is rotated inwards or outwards respectively.

The Air Lever. Above the throttle twist-grip is a short lever which also regulates the mixture by controlling the amount of air supplied to the Amal semi-automatic carburettor. For practical purposes this control lever, which like the throttle opens inwards, is only used for starting when it should be fully closed. At all other times it should be kept wide open.

The Ignition Lever. In a position corresponding to the air lever but at the opposite side of the handlebars (pre-1949, 1955-8 models) is a lever which advances or retards the spark at the plug to compensate for increases in engine revolutions by inward or

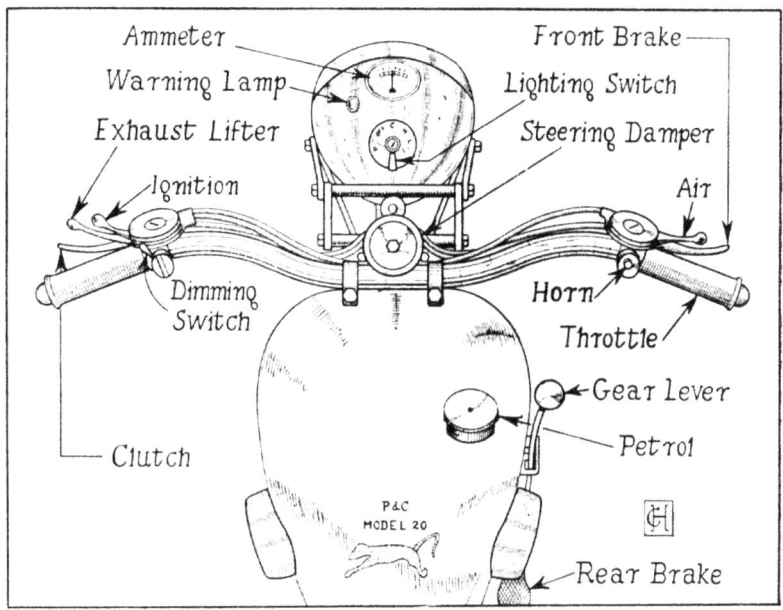

Fig. 2. The Panther Control Layout (Pre-1949)

The general arrangement is similar on all models, but on pre-1936 machines trigger-type levers were used for some of the engine controls. On "Maglita" models there is, of course, no warning lamp and a steering damper is fitted only on the 1936 Model 70. 1945-8 models have foot gear-change

outward movement respectively (reversed 1932-37, 1955-8). This lever is kept fully advanced except when starting up and when the engine shows signs of knocking, in which case it is slightly retarded.

Ignition Switch. On coil-ignition models it is important to disconnect the battery from the coil when leaving the machine standing so as to avoid wastage of current. An ignition switch is therefore necessary, and this is combined with the lighting switch. When this switch is in the "Off" position, the ignition is not switched off until the detachable ignition key is turned.

The Exhaust-valve Lifter. The exhaust-valve lifter is situated close to the clutch lever, and its sole objects are to facilitate starting by enabling the engine to be kicked over compression (with the exhaust valve raised) and to enable the engine to be stopped. Using the lifter for controlling speed is cruelty to the engine.

The Gear Lever. This lever which is mounted beside the petrol tank or else direct on the gearbox (in the case of foot control) is primarily designed to enable the ratio of the engine to the rear wheel speed to be varied according to the amount of work the engine has to do, so saving unduly stressing both the engine and transmission when moving off, hill climbing, etc. There are three or four speeds, first gear giving the lowest road-speed on the level. Gear changes are effected by coupling up different size gear-wheels in the gearbox, and as one set of gear wheels is on a shaft connected (by chain) to the rear wheel and another set on a shaft connected (by chain) to the engine, before a gear change can be accomplished obviously we must disconnect the engine. This is done by means of the clutch. A gear-change indicator is a modern fitment.

The Clutch. A long lever on the left-hand side of the handlebars is used to release the clutch friction-plates and so disconnect the engine from the gearbox (mainshaft). This lever must always be brought fully into play before attempting to move the gear lever. This is very important. "NEUTRAL" is a position of the gear lever in which the engine is disconnected from the gearbox (layshaft) *inside* the gearbox. Raising the clutch has the same effect, but it is tiring and dangerous to allow the machine to stand for long with the engine running and the clutch out. In the garage the gear lever should at all times be kept in neutral.

The Brakes. These need no explanation, but it should be mentioned that their use should be as sparing as possible. By controlling speed on the throttle, wear of the transmission and tyres is reduced to the minimum. For light braking, use the rear brake pedal alone, but normally both should be applied simultaneously. Police are now empowered to test brakes.

Starting Up the Engine. Having understood the action of the controls and moved them about, you should now be competent to start up the engine and get on the road for the first time. This first trip is always regarded by the "tyro" with something approaching awe. Any preliminary nervousness, however, disappears almost instantly on taking the road, and confidence is gradually, and then rapidly, acquired. Thereafter progress is very rapid indeed, and after about a dozen runs or so the rider usually feels capable of undertaking his first long cross-country trip, and begins thoroughly to enjoy the sport. But the rider should guard against becoming prematurely over-confident of his own abilities, and keep his speed down to reasonable proportions for some considerable time. It is a well-known fact and proved by insurance statistics that one of the most risky periods in a motor-cyclist's life is when he has just got real confidence but lacks real experience. *Do not take such risks, please.*

Before starting up, first verify that the gear lever is in neutral

FIG. 3. AN ATTRACTIVE O.H.V. "THREE-FIFTY"—THE 1958 PANTHER MODEL 75 SPRINGER

This 350 c.c. magneto-ignition model with green-and-chromium tank has a Burman four-speed gearbox, "swinging arm" rear suspension (Armstrong), full width light-alloy front hub, etc. It will touch 75 m.p.h., and fuel and oil consumptions average about 100 m.p.g. and 2000 m.p.g. respectively. The 250 c.c. coil-ignition Model 65 is similar and magneto-ignition and a full width light-alloy front hub are available as extras. Both models have a box-type air filter and saddle, but a dual seat is available as an extra

and the petrol turned on.* Then flood the carburettor slightly by *gently* depressing the float chamber "tickler" and adjust the controls for starting which is really an acquired knack. Hard-and-fast rules do not apply to all machines and variations in temperature affect the best setting. Roughly speaking, however, when starting *from cold* the throttle twist-grip should be opened very slightly (about one-eighth), the air lever closed completely and the ignition lever (pre-1949, 1955–8 Model 75) half advanced. The same setting is applicable for starting a warm engine, but the air lever should be opened slightly; do not "flood."

* Open *one* tap only. Keep the other tap shut to maintain a reserve supply of petrol.

New engines are inclined to be rather stiff, and to free the piston it is advisable to turn the engine over several times with the exhaust-valve lifter raised, air lever shut, and the throttle nearly closed. On coil-ignition models now switch on the ignition.

To start the engine, stand astride the machine, turn the engine till resistance is felt on compression, raise the exhaust-valve lifter momentarily, turn the engine over a fraction more, release the exhaust-valve lifter, and then rotate the engine fast with a long swinging kick. With the engine and carburettor in proper order, a start should be effected on the third kick at the most. Failure to start quickly is usually due to some definite defect, and generally ignition trouble; the plug should be removed, inspected, and, if necessary, cleaned and the points adjusted. (See page 47.)

Warming Up the Engine. Once the engine has sprung into life, adjust the controls to give a sweet "pilot" tick-over, and resist the temptation to "rev" it up *until the oil is circulating properly and has warmed up.* Any engine racing, especially when not under load, is most injurious. Also avoid very slow running, as this causes low-temperature condensation.

Moving Off. Raise the clutch (when both gearbox mainshaft and layshaft become idle), place the gear lever in first gear, and allow the transmission to take up the drive by progressively and gently letting-in the clutch, when the machine will move off. As it picks up speed, advance the ignition lever fully (pre-1949, 1955-8 Model 75), give full air and slightly more throttle.

If any difficulty is experienced in engaging first gear, it is in all probability due to the clutch plates not freeing properly (in the case of machines with aluminium chain-case). The engine should be stopped, the clutch withdrawn, and if the rider gives a sharp dig to the kick-starter it will free the plates. It is a good plan to make a practice of doing this always before starting the engine.

Change from First to Second Gear. The knack of gear-changing on a motor-cycle is rapidly mastered, and gear crashing of a serious nature is impossible owing to the special design of the Burman gearbox, where all pinions are of the constant-mesh type. Speed up the machine until about 12 m.p.h. is attained, declutch, and simultaneously throttle down the engine, wait a second until mainshaft and layshaft are running at the same speed, and push gear lever home, afterwards letting in the clutch gently and throttling up again to take the increased load. *Never employ force on the gear lever.* All operations should be quick but accurate, and progressive, and *no attempt should ever be made to change gear without first declutching. On no account allow the engine to knock* (i.e. make a metallic noise) by driving too slowly under load or with too advanced ignition-timing (pre-1949, 1955–8 Model 75).

Change from Second to Third Gear. Proceed as before. Speed up the machine until it has plenty of momentum, declutch, throttle down, wait a second and smartly move the gear lever home into third gear, afterwards throttling up again until the desired speed is reached. On a four-speed model change similarly into top gear.

Be Careful with Foot Control. The foot-control lever has a very considerable leverage and, to avoid damage to the gear selectors and control mechanism, it must not be used roughly. When changing gear, depress or raise the lever *gently and fully*, according to whether you are changing up or down respectively, by movement of the toe, and do not lift the foot from the pedal *until the clutch has been re-engaged*. Also remember that the lever always returns to the *same position* after every gear change. Neutral is between first and second gear, as shown on the indicator.

Change From Top to First Gear. Throttle down until the machine is travelling at a speed at which it normally does in first gear, lift the clutch and move the gear lever into first-gear position. With foot control the lever can be raised twice or three times in quick succession (three- or four-speed gearbox respectively).

To Stop. Close the throttle, apply the two brakes, whip out the clutch and go into bottom gear, opening the throttle again slightly so as to prevent the engine from stopping. A little practice will soon enable you to execute this apparently complicated manoeuvre with lightning speed, which is so necessary in emergency. Practise stopping and gear changing on quiet roads until you feel skilled enough to venture on to busy thoroughfares, and go out on the machine every day if possible until you have acquired some confidence. Run with the headlamp switch in the "C" ("Off," 1949–58) position. Then when you have become efficient, have digested the Highway Code, and know something about the Law, you can undertake your first cross-country run.

After a Run. Be sure to turn the ignition off by means of the small ignition key in the case of a coil-ignition model, otherwise, if the contacts of the contact-breaker happen to be closed, the battery may discharge when the machine is left standing. In the case of "Maglita" models it does not, of course, matter whether the headlamp switch is turned to the "Off" or "C" position.

Watch the "Warning" Lamp. This small red lamp, which is mounted in or close to the ammeter on coil-ignition models, warns you regarding the question of turning off the ignition mentioned above. As the engine slows down the lamp will be found to brighten, and when you stop the engine with the ignition left on it will remain illuminated *if the contacts happen to be closed*. Make a habit of always switching off the ignition.

To Prevent Theft. If you own a coil-ignition model and sometimes leave the machine in such a place that it could be stolen, you can minimize the risk by turning the ignition off by means of the ignition key which fits the slot in the centre of the headlamp switch. Do not forget to *remove* the key. (See also page 112.)

Use of Headlamp Switch. To prevent a low state of charge of the battery, always run during the day-time (see also page 112) for the first few hours with the switch in the "C" position. The Miller switch which has a half-charge resistance, has on Red Panther coil-ignition models the following five positions—

P—Headlamp (pilot bulb) and tail light; no charge from the dynamo.
"Off"—Lamps off and dynamo not charging.
C—Dynamo charging (½ max.).
H—Headlamp (main bulb) and tail light, with dynamo on full charge.
L—Headlamp (pilot bulb) and tail light, dynamo on full charge.

The switch positions on "Maglita" Red Panthers are as above, but there is not an ignition key, and the "Parking" position is omitted, the "L" position sufficing.

On all 1939-58 models with Miller or Lucas compensated voltage control, the lighting switch positions are—

"Off"—All lamps off.
L—Headlamp (pilot bulb) and rear lamp on.
H—Headlamp (main bulb) and rear lamp on.

With the switch in any of the above three positions, the dynamo charges the battery according to its state of charge and the lamp load (see page 112). On the coil-ignition Models 65 and 65 de Luxe, a detachable ignition key (see page 3) is provided in the centre of the lighting switch, with positions marked "Off," "Low," and "High."

The Ammeter. With the switch in the "C" position the ammeter needle should show a charge of 3-4 amp. and 2-3 amp. respectively in the case of Miller coil, and "Maglita" models. (See page 112.)

Do Not Exceed Half Throttle for 500 Miles. If you wish to get the best out of your Panther for years to come, be very careful during the first 500 miles. Do not allow the engine to labour (change down if necessary) and go steady with the twist-grip. Half throttle should *never* be exceeded during the first 500 miles and 30 m.p.h. during the first 200 miles. Take it from the author—this advice is *very* important. During the running-in period use the gearbox as much as possible and should a new engine "pull up," immediately declutch and close the throttle. It is a good plan during the running-in period to add a "shot" of upper cylinder lubricant (such as Redex) to each gallon of petrol.

FIG. 4. THE 248, 348 C.C. RED PANTHER

This machine, with inclined O.H.V. push-rod engine, was popular during the period 1932-9 and the 250 c.c. model cost only £29 17s. 6d. new! It was the forerunner of the present attractive range of vertical engine lightweights

Run on a Good Plug. Suitable plugs for 250, 350 c.c. models are the 18 mm., Lodge H3, Champion 16, or K.L.G. M.60, and the 14 mm., Lodge HN or H14, Champion L-10S or K.L.G. F.70. See also page 11, paragraph 7.

Why Tyre Pressures are Important. If they are not "just so," the tyres will suffer, riding will lack comfort, steering may be difficult and the machine may get a "skidding complex." The way to avoid such drawbacks is to check the pressures regularly *with a pressure gauge* and inflate as required. On 348 c.c. models give 20 lb. per sq. in. front and 20 lb. per sq. in. rear. On 248 c.c. models give 16 lb. per sq. in. for the front tyre, and 18 lb. per sq. in. for the rear tyre. If you carry human luggage at the back, add about 4 lb. per sq. in. to rear pressure. Remember smooth tyres are now illegal.

The Essence of Good Driving. A good driver, besides respecting the rights of other road users and conforming to the Law, invariably indicates to other traffic clearly and in *ample time* his intended movements which he does with as little fuss as possible. He also avoids excessive noise and rides in a state of constantly expecting the unexpected. In other words, he uses his "grey matter" and develops what is commonly called road sense. This sense is only acquired thoroughly after extensive driving experience, but there is no reason why *you* should not become a first-class driver, and today the public expects it.

A Useful Book for Panther Owners. A book written by the author and likely to be of interest to riders of Panther lightweights, especially novices, is *The Art of Motor-cycling* (Pitman). This covers comprehensively riding comfort, roadworthiness, accessories, clothing, shields, engine principles, learning to ride, the technique of riding, the driving test, legal matters, insurance, preliminaries, etc.

In this maintenance handbook it is only possible to give a very brief outline of essential preliminaries. When buying a new or second-hand machine from a dealer, it is generally found that the dealer will attend personally to many of the preliminaries, but in other cases it is necessary to deal with them oneself.

Outline of Essential Preliminaries. You are not allowed by law to ride a motor-cycle on the public highway until you have complied with certain preliminaries. You must—

1. Take out an insurance policy to cover all *third-party* risks, and obtain the vital "certificate of insurance." With a brand new machine obtain a "cover note" pending the allocation of a registration number and the issue of the insurance policy and the "certificate." If your Panther is worth a considerable sum, it is obviously desirable to take out full comprehensive insurance. Should you purchase the machine new on deferred terms, you will have no option in the matter.

2. Obtain the registration book and the registration licence (Form R.F. 1/2*), or renew the licence (Form R.F. 1/A). All 250 c.c. and 350 c.c. Panthers are taxed at the rate of £1 17s. 6d. and £3 15s. per annum respectively. If a sidecar is attached (not recommended), the additional tax required is £1 5s. per annum.

3. Obtain a provisional (six months), an annual, or a long-term (see page 11) driving licence (Form D.L. 1.). The driving licence

* On Form R.F. 1/2 (required for original registration or change of ownership) you must state the engine and frame markings situated on the near side of the oil sump and on the near side of the saddle lug just below the saddle respectively.

must immediately be *signed*. Note that you are not eligible for an annual or long-term driving licence (for group C) until you are sixteen and have also complied with *one* of the following conditions—

(*a*) You have held a licence (other than a provisional or visitor's licence) authorizing the driving of vehicles of the class or description applied for *within a period of* 10 *years ending on the date of coming into force of the licence applied for*, or

(*b*) You have passed the prescribed driving test (this includes a test passed whilst serving in H.M. Forces) *during the said period of* 10 *years*.

4. If not already provided, fit a red reflector (of $1\frac{1}{2}$ in. minimum diameter) vertically at the rear of the motor-cycle, and in the case of a sidecar outfit an additional red reflector at the rear of the sidecar and at the same height as the reflector on the motor-cycle.

5. Mount "L" plates at the front and rear, if you are eligible for a provisional licence only.

6. If you hold only a provisional licence and carry a pillion passenger, see that he or she holds a current annual or substantive driving-licence for Group C.

7. Use an ignition-suppression type sparking plug or terminal cover if the machine was registered for the first time after 1st July, 1953, so as not to cause interference to television and radio sets.

Note that all the official forms previously referred to are obtainable from a money-order post office.

Long-term Driving Licences. Note that substantive driving licences lasting *three years* and costing 15s. are now obtainable by all riders who hold a "provisional" licence and satisfactorily complete their driving test. For other riders, with surnames beginning A–F, a three-year driving licence has been available since 1st September, 1957, subject to the satisfactory completion of Form D.L.1 (see page 10, paragraph 3). Those with surnames beginning G–O can obtain a three-year licence from September 1st, 1958. The remaining riders, with surnames starting P–Z will have to wait until 1st September, 1959, until they can obtain a three-year licence instead of an annual licence.

CHAPTER II
TUNING THE CARBURETTOR

A STANDARD type Amal needle-jet carburettor is fitted to all 1932–55 single-cylinder 250 c.c. and 350 c.c. Panther engines but all 1956 and later engines have the "Monobloc" type Amal needle-jet carburettor fitted.

AMAL STANDARD CARBURETTOR

An understanding of the working of the standard Amal carburettor is desirable before considering its tuning and maintenance. Referring to Fig. 5, showing a sectional view of the Amal semi-automatic carburettor, (A) is the carburettor body or mixing chamber, the upper part of which has a throttle valve (B), with taper needle (C) attached by a needle clip. The throttle valve regulates the quantity of mixture supplied to the engine. Passing through the valve is the air valve (D), independently operated and serving the purpose of obstructing the main air-passage for starting and mixture regulation. Fixed to the underside of the mixing chamber by the union nut (E) is the jet block (F), and interposed between them is a fibre washer to ensure a petrol-tight joint.

On the upper part of the block is the jet-block barrel (H), forming a clean through-way. Integral with the jet block is the pilot jet (J), supplied through the passage (K). The adjustable pilot-air intake (L) communicates with a chamber, from which issues the pilot outlet (M) and the by-pass (N). A throttle stop (see Fig. 6) is provided on the mixing chamber, by which the position of the throttle valve for tick-over is regulated independently of the cable adjustment.

The needle jet (O) is screwed in the underside of the jet block, and carries at its bottom end the main jet (P). Both these jets are removable when the jet plug (Q), which bolts the mixing chamber and the float chamber together, is removed. The float chamber, which has bottom feed, consists of a cup (R) fed with petrol through union (S). It contains the float (T) and the needle valve (U) attached by the clip (V). The float-chamber cover (W) has a lock screw (X) for security.

The petrol tap having been turned on, petrol will flow past the needle valve (U) until the quantity of petrol in the chamber (R) is sufficient to raise the float (T), when the needle valve (U) will prevent a further supply entering the float chamber until some in the chamber has already been used up by the engine. The float

TUNING THE CARBURETTOR 13

chamber having filled to its correct level, the fuel passes along the
passages through the diagonal holes in the jet plug (*Q*), when it will
be in communication with the main jet (*P*) and the pilot feed-hole

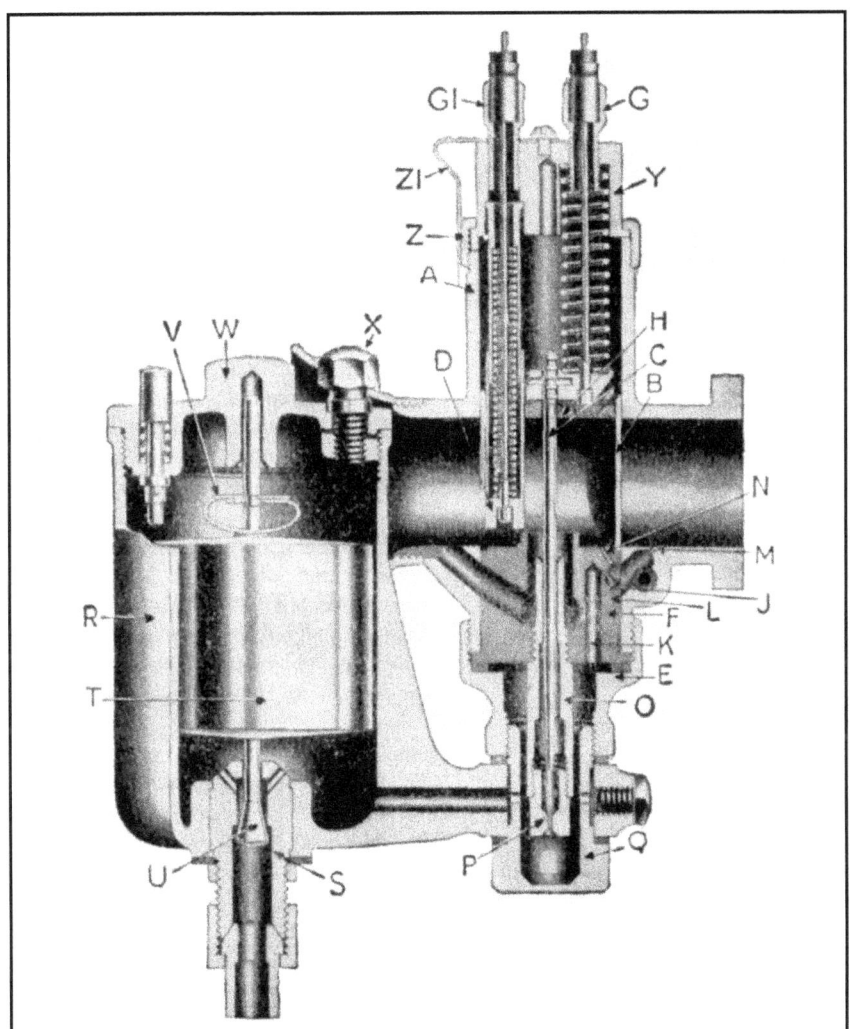

FIG. 5. SECTIONAL VIEW OF AMAL STANDARD NEEDLE-JET
CARBURETTOR FITTED TO ALL 1932-55 250 C.C., 350 C.C. PANTHERS

(*K*); the level in the needle and pilot jets is, obviously, the
same as that maintained in the float chamber.

Imagine the throttle valve (*B*) very slightly open. As the piston
descends, a partial vacuum is created in the carburettor, causing
a rush of air through the pilot-air hole (*L*) and drawing fuel from the

pilot jet (J). The mixture of air and fuel is admitted to the engine through the pilot outlet (M) which has a pilot-air screw adjustment (see Fig. 6), used in conjunction with the throttle-stop screw to obtain a good slow running mixture. The quantity of mixture capable of being passed by the pilot outlet (M) is insufficient to run the engine. This mixture also carries excess of fuel. Consequently, before a combustible mixture is admitted, throttle valve (B) must be slightly raised, admitting further air from the main air-intake.

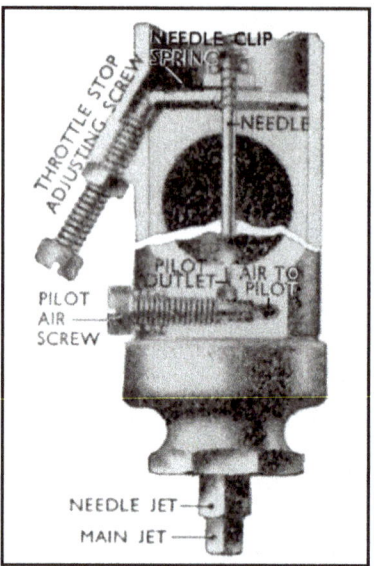

Fig. 6. Throttle Stop and Pilot-air Screw
(Standard Carburettor)

The farther the throttle valve is opened, the less will be the depression on the outlet (M), but, in turn, a higher depression will be created on the by-pass (N), and the pilot mixture will flow from this passage as well as from the outlet M.

The mixture supplied by the pilot and by-pass system is supplemented at about one-eighth throttle by fuel from the main jet (P), the throttle valve cut-away determining the mixture strength from here to one-quarter throttle.

Proceeding up the throttle range, mixture control by the needle position occurs from one-quarter to three-quarters throttle, and from this point the main jet is the only regulation.

The air valve (D), which is cable-operated on the standard carburettor, has the effect of obstructing the main through-way and, in consequence, increasing the depression on the main jet, enriching the mixture. Two cable adjusters (G), ($G1$), are provided.

Key to Fig. 7

1. Mixing-chamber cap.
2. Mixing-chamber cap ring.
3. Air valve.
4. Jet-needle clip.
5. Jet block.
6. Air passage to pilot jet.
7. Tickler assembly.
8. Banjo securing-bolt.
9. Float needle.
10. Float.
11. Float-chamber cover screws.
12. Float-chamber cover.
13. Float chamber.
14. Needle jet.
15. Main-jet holder.
16. Main jet.
17. Pilot jet.
18. Throttle-stop adjusting screw.
19. Jet block locating-screw.
20. Pilot-air adjusting screw.
21. Mixing chamber.
22. Fibre seal.
23. Jet needle.
24. Throttle valve.
25. Throttle return-spring.

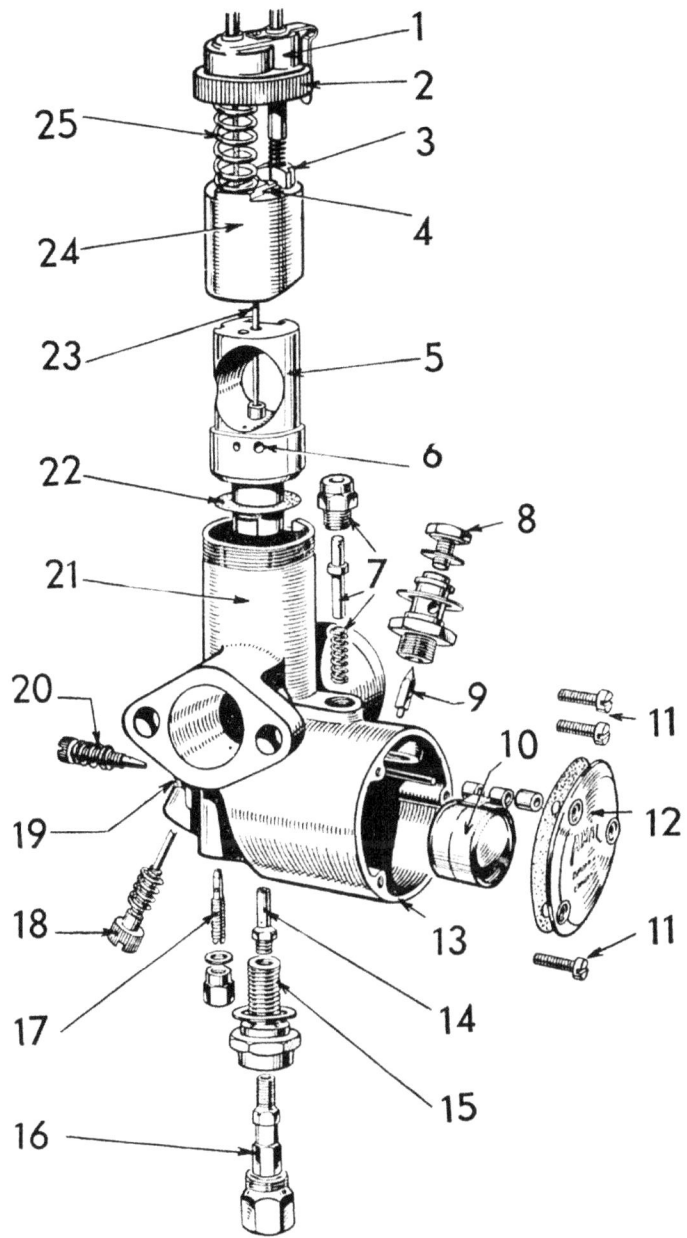

Fig. 7. Amal "Monobloc" Carburettor (1956 onwards) shown dismantled
(*By courtesy of B.S.A. Motor Cycles, Ltd.*)

AMAL "MONOBLOC" CARBURETTOR

The Amal "Monobloc" carburettor specified on all 1956 and later Panther O.H.V. singles differs from the standard type, used before 1956, in several respects. But its general functioning is similar. The "Monobloc" design includes: a horizontal float chamber made integral with the carburettor body: a float needle of moulded nylon; a top petrol feed; a needle jet with bleed holes giving two-way compensation; and a detachable pilot jet which can be easily cleaned.

Fig. 7 shows all the essential parts of the instrument. The float chamber (13) and needle (9) maintain a constant level of petrol in the needle jet (14) and the pilot jet (17). The selection by the makers of the appropriate jet sizes and main-bore choke ensures a proper atomizing and proportioning of the petrol and air sucked into the engine.

The air valve (3) is normally kept fully raised, and the throttle valve (24) controlled by the handlebar twist-grip controls the volume of mixture, and therefore the power. At all throttle openings a correct mixture is automatically obtained.

The "Monobloc" carburettor, like the standard instrument, operates in four stages. When opening the throttle from the fully closed position to one-eighth open (for tick-over) the mixture is supplied by the pilot jet (17), and the strength of the mixture is determined by the setting of the knurled pilot-air adjusting screw (20) which has a coil locking-spring to facilitate adjustment. As the throttle is opened slightly farther, the main jet system comes into action, the mixture being augmented by the main jet (16) through the pilot by-pass.

The amount of cut-away on the atmospheric side of the throttle valve regulates the petrol-to-air ratio between one-eighth and one-quarter throttle. The needle jet (14) and the jet needle (23) take over the mixture regulation between one-quarter and three-quarter throttle, and the mixture strength is determined by the relative position of the needle in the clip (4) attached to the throttle valve (24). When the throttle is opened beyond three-quarters, the mixture strength is determined only by the size of the main jet. Note that the main jet (16) does not spray petrol direct into the carburettor mixing-chamber, but discharges through the needle jet into the primary air-chamber. From there it enters the main choke through the primary air-choke. The latter has a two way compensating action in conjunction with the "bleed" holes in the needle jet. Pilot and main jet behaviour are not affected by this two-way compensation which governs only acceleration at normal cruising speed.

On the "Monobloc" carburettor petrol consumption is better than on the standard type instrument; general performance is good.

TUNING AMAL CARBURETTOR (STANDARD AND "MONOBLOC" TYPES)

The same tuning instructions apply to the standard and "Monobloc" instruments. Normally *it is unwise to interfere with the maker's carburettor setting* (see below) unless there is a very special reason for doing so. However, it is sometimes desirable to make a slow-running adjustment with the pilot-air adjusting screw and throttle-stop screw.

To vary the strength of the running mixture (rarely necessary), it is necessary to adjust the height of the needle in the throttle valve, or else to fit a larger or smaller size main jet. The condition of the sparking plug provides an excellent guide to the condition of the mixture.

Slow-running Adjustment Procedure. This should be effected with the engine already *warmed up*. If the adjustment is appreciably at fault, screw home the pilot-air adjusting screw fully and then unscrew it (usually about two complete turns) until the engine idles at an excessive speed, with the throttle twist-grip closed and the throttle slide abutting the throttle-stop screw. The air lever should be fully open and the ignition lever (where automatic ignition-advance is not provided) should be set to obtain the best slow-running (half to two thirds advanced).

AMAL CARBURETTOR SETTINGS FOR 1932–55 PANTHERS

Panther Model	Main Jet Size	Throttle Slide	Needle Jet	Needle Position
1932–9 250 c.c.	80	4/5	Std.	Groove 3
1945–55 250 c.c.	90	4/5	Std.	Groove 3
1932–53 350 c.c.	110	5/4	Std.	Groove 3
1954–5 350 c.c.	160	6/4	Std.	Groove 3

AMAL CARBURETTOR SETTINGS FOR 1956–8 PANTHERS
(With Panther Box-type Air Filter Fitted)

Panther Model	Main Jet Size	Pilot Jet Size	Throttle Valve	Needle Position
1956–8 250 c.c.	120	30	375/4	3
1956–8 350 c.c.	180	30	376/4	2

Loosen the nut (omitted on the "Monobloc" carburettor) securing the throttle-stop screw, and unscrew the latter until the engine slows up and begins to falter. Then screw the pilot-air adjusting screw in or out as required to enable the engine to run regularly and faster. To weaken the mixture, screw the pilot-air adjusting screw *outwards*.

Slowly lower the throttle-stop screw until the engine again begins to falter. Then lock the throttle-stop screw (standard carburettor) with the lock-nut and reset the pilot-air adjusting screw to obtain the best slow-running. If after making this second adjustment the engine ticks over too fast, repeat the adjustment a third time. The combined adjustment sounds complicated but in practice is quite simple. It is important to avoid excessive richness of the slow-running mixture, especially if much riding is done on small throttle openings; if the mixture is too rich, considerable running on the pilot jet will occur while riding, with consequently a high fuel consumption.

Aim at obtaining the best tick-over, preferably on a mixture just bordering on the weak side. The engine should be on the point of spitting-back.* When perfect slow-running has been obtained, tighten the locknut (standard carburettor) on the throttle-stop screw without disturbing the position of the screw.

Pilot Jet Obstructed. If the adjustment of the pilot jet does not obtain the desired results and the engine will not idle nicely with the throttle almost closed, the air lever fully open, and the ignition lever (where fitted) half to two-thirds advanced, it is possible that the pilot jet is obstructed. The jet passage (on the standard carburettor a duct drilled in the jet block) is very small and can readily become choked.

To gain access to the pilot jet on the standard carburettor (see Fig. 5), remove the jet plug (Q) and the float chamber (R), and then detach the jet block (F) by pushing or tapping it out of the mixing chamber. The pilot jet (J) can then be cleared by blowing through it, or by means of a *very* fine strand of wire.

With the "Monobloc" carburettor (see Fig. 7) to remove the pilot jet (17), remove the pilot jet cover-nut and then unscrew the jet itself which should be thoroughly cleaned in petrol and then blown through. See that the air passage (6) to the pilot jet, and also the pilot outlet, are quite clear.

Poor Slow-running. If it is found impossible to obtain good slow-running by making the pilot-air adjustment as described on page 17, it is probable that some defect other than carburation

---

* Rev the engine up and down sharply several times (while at rest and while riding) and note whether the exhaust is nice and crisp, with no "flat spots" as the twist-grip is turned. It is essential to combine good tick-over with good acceleration.

TUNING THE CARBURETTOR

is responsible for preventing the engine running slowly at low revolutions. Air leaks or badly-seating valves may weaken the mixture. Defects in the ignition system may also be responsible for poor tick-over. The sparking plug may be oily, or the points set too close (see page 47). Possibly the spark is excessively advanced or the contact-breaker needs attention (see pages 84-7). Examine the slip ring for oil and see that the pick-up brush is bedding down and in good condition. Also examine the H.T. cable for signs of shorting.

High Fuel Consumption. If in spite of careful checking on the tuning of the carburettor, high fuel consumption continues, it is likely that one or more of several causes is responsible for wastage of precious fuel. Late ignition timing will eat into your petrol supplies quickly. The same applies to poor engine compression due to badly-fitting piston rings or valves. Also take into consideration the question of flooding due to a faulty float, air leakage at the joint between the carburettor and the engine, weak valve springs. See that no wastage is caused by slack petrol pipe union-nuts.

CARBURETTOR MAINTENANCE

To ensure correct carburation it is advisable occasionally to remove the carburettor from the engine, strip it down completely, and then thoroughly clean it. It is a good plan to do this about every six months as described below.

To Dismantle Standard Carburettor. First disconnect the air filter (where fitted) then close both petrol taps and disconnect the twin petrol pipes from the carburettor by undoing the single union-nut at the base of the float chamber. Referring to Fig. 5, loosen the jet plug (Q) and slacken the mixing chamber union-nut (E).

Unscrew the mixing chamber knurled cap-ring (Z) held by the retaining spring ($Z1$) at the top of the carburettor, and remove the two nuts securing the carburettor flange to the face of the inlet port. Now remove the body of the carburettor, complete with the float chamber, from the engine.

When removing the carburettor, pull the air valve (D) and the throttle valve (B), together with the jet needle (C), from the mixing chamber (A); temporarily tie up the slides out of the way. It is not necessary to remove the air and throttle slides from the control cables unless it is desired to renew the slides or control cables. The jet needle (C) can be adjusted for position in, or removed from, the throttle slide by removing the spring clip from the top of the slide. Examine the carburettor-flange washer, and if damaged, renew it.

With the carburettor removed from the engine, proceed to remove the jet plug (*Q*) and the float chamber (*R*). Also remove the main jet (*P*) and the needle jet (*O*). Then completely unscrew the mixing-chamber union-nut (*E*) and push the jet block (*F*) right out; if stiff, tap the jet block out gently with a wooden stump. Unscrew the float-chamber cover (*W*) after loosening the locking screw (*X*). Then withdraw the float by pinching the clip (*V*) inwards, and pull gently upwards.

To Dismantle "Monobloc" Carburettor. Disconnect the air filter (where fitted). Close both petrol taps and disconnect the twin petrol pipes by undoing the banjo bolt (8) over the float chamber (see Fig. 7). Referring to Fig. 7, unscrew the mixing chamber knurled cap-ring (2) on top of the carburetor and remove the two nuts securing the carburettor flange to the face of the inlet port. Then remove the body of the carburettor (21), complete with the integral float chamber (13). While removing the carburettor, pull the air valve (3) and the throttle valve (24) from the mixing chamber and tie them up temporarily out of the way. As mentioned in the instructions for the standard type carburettor, it is rarely necessary to disconnect the slides from the cables. Check that the flange washer is sound.

Further dismantling is straightforward. Referring to Fig. 7, to remove the jet needle (23), withdraw the jet-needle clip (4) on top of the throttle valve, and remove the needle. To obtain access to the float (10), remove the three screws (11) securing the float-chamber cover (12). Lift out the hinged float (10) and withdraw the moulded-nylon needle (9). Lay both aside for cleaning. The float-chamber vent, by the way, is embodied in the tickler assembly (7), and the top-feed union houses a filter element of fine gauze which is rapidly accessible for cleaning.

To remove the main jet (16), remove the main-jet cover and unscrew the jet from the jet holder (15), which should also be unscrewed. Remove the jet-block locating screw (19) to the left of and slightly below the pilot-air adjusting screw. Then push or tap out the jet block (5) and fibre seal (22) through the large end of the mixing chamber (21). To remove the pilot jet (17), remove the pilot-jet cover nut and unscrew the jet.

Cleaning Carburettor. Wash all the carburettor components, thoroughly clean with petrol and blow through the various ducts and passages to make sure they are quite clear. Avoid using a fluffy rag for drying purposes. Pay special attention to the small pilot-jet passages in the jet block on both the standard and "Monobloc" type instruments. See that all impurities are removed from inside the float chamber. On the "Monobloc" carburettor do not

TUNING THE CARBURETTOR

forget to clean the detachable pilot jet and the filter gauze inside the top-feed union for the float chamber.

Inspecting Components. When dismantling the carburettor it is advisable to make a close inspection of the various parts if the carburettor has been in continuous service for a considerable period. Clean all components thoroughly.

1. THE FLOAT CHAMBER. Examine the components very carefully and check that the vent is unobstructed. The float must be in perfect condition. Clean the moulded-nylon needle on the "Monobloc" carburettor very thoroughly, and be careful not to damage it. On a standard carburettor hand-polish the valve part of the float needle by rotating the needle on its seat while pulling it vertically upwards. If a distinct shoulder is visible on the needle where it seats, renew the needle at once. Check for any sign of bending or distortion of the clip (see Fig. 8).

2. THE THROTTLE VALVE. Test this for fit in the mixing chamber. Should excessive play exist, renew the slide forthwith. See that the new slide has the correct amount of cut-away.

3. THE JET-NEEDLE CLIP. The spring clip securing the tapered needle to the throttle valve must grip the needle firmly, and free rotation must *not* occur, as this causes the needle groove to wear. Always be careful to replace the needle with the clip in the correct groove (see Table on page 17).

4. THE JET BLOCK. Before tapping this home in the mixing chamber verify by blowing that the pilot-jet ducts are clear and that the jet-block fibre seal is in good condition.

5. THE CARBURETTOR FLANGE. Examine this for truth with a straightedge. Distortion sometimes occurs, and this may cause an air leak. If the flange is slightly concave, file and rub down the face with emery cloth until it is dead flat and smooth.

Assembling Standard Carburettor. Referring to Fig. 5, refit the jet block (F) with the fibre washer on its under-side, and screw on lightly the mixing-chamber union nut (E). Screw in the needle jet (O) and the main jet (P). Open the air lever $\frac{7}{8}$ in. and the throttle twist-grip half way; grasp the air slide between the thumb and the finger and make sure that the jet needle enters the central hole in the barrel (H). Slightly turn the throttle slide until it enters the barrel guide, when on pushing down the slides, the air valve should enter its guide. If not, slightly move the mixing chamber cap (Y), when the air valve will slide into position. Screw home the mixing-chamber knurled cap-ring (Z). No force is necessary.

Replace the carburettor-flange washer, offer up the carburettor body and secure in position by tightening the two nuts evenly.

Replace the float and needle in the float chamber, holding the needle against its seating with a pencil until the float (*T*) and needle clip (*V*) are slipped into position. See that the spring clip enters the needle groove. Then screw home the float-chamber cover securely and lock in position by tightening lock-screw (*X*).

Insert the jet plug (*Q*) in the union nut (*E*) and very firmly tighten the union nut with a suitable spanner. Remove the jet plug, fit the float chamber, and secure with the jet plug. Be sure there is a fibre washer above and below the float-chamber lug as

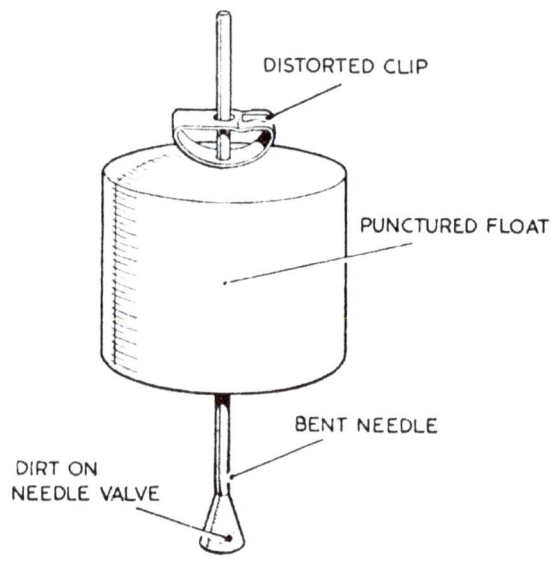

FIG. 8. CAUSES OF " FLOODING " (STD. CARBURETTOR)

shown in Fig. 5. When the float chamber has been correctly positioned, tighten the jet plug firmly. Finally reconnect the twin petrol pipes and tighten the union nut at the base of the float chamber. Replace the air filter (where provided). If the pilot-jet adjustment is disturbed, re-tune as described on page 17.

Jet-needle Wear. The needle itself does *not* wear, though some wear of the groove may occur if the jet-needle clip is not grasping the needle firmly. If the mixture is too rich with the clip in No. 1 groove (nearest the top), it is probable that the needle jet needs to be renewed because of wear. It is assumed that the carburettor is correctly tuned and maintained.

To Assemble "Monobloc" Carburettor. Do this in the reverse order of dismantling. Referring to Fig. 7, screw home the pilot

TUNING THE CARBURETTOR

jet (17) and the pilot jet cover-nut, not omitting to replace its washer. Push or tap home the jet block (5) and fibre-seal (22) through the large end of the mixing chamber (21). Check that the fibre-seal fitted to the stub of the jet block is in good condition. Then fit the jet block locating-screw (19). Screw the main-jet holder (15) into the jet block; check that the washer for the holder is sound. Next screw the main jet (16) into the jet holder.

Replace the moulded-nylon needle (9) in the float chamber (13), and fit the hinged float (10) with the *narrow* side of the hinge uppermost. Afterwards fit the float-chamber cover (12) and secure by means of the three screws (11). Verify that the cover, and body faces are undamaged and quite clean. Renew the washer.

If previously removed, attach the jet needle (23) to the throttle valve (24) and secure with the jet-needle clip (4), making sure that the clip enters the correct groove. (See Table on page 17.)

Position the carburettor-flange washer, and offer up the carburettor to the face of the inlet port after easing the air and throttle valves (3) and (24) down into the mixing chamber (see hints on page 21 concerning the standard carburettor). When easing the throttle valve home, make sure that the tapered jet-needle (23) really enters the hole in the jet block (5). Secure the carburettor flange firmly to the engine by means of the two nuts, and tighten these evenly. Tighten down firmly the mixing-chamber knurled cap-ring (2) and see that the throttle slide works freely.

Finally reconnect the twin petrol pipes by tightening the banjo bolt (8) over the float chamber (13). Also reconnect the air filter.

The Vokes Air Filter (Pre-1956). The filter element requires to be renewed only at intervals of 10,000 miles, but the element should be cleaned regularly every 2000 miles. Wash the three-ply element thoroughly in petrol, allow to dry, and then submerge it in clean engine oil (grade SAE 20) for a few minutes. Allow the surplus oil to drain off for about fifteen minutes, and then reassemble.

The P. & M. Air Filter (1956 Onwards). This includes a large filter element of woven yarn and fine wire, fitted between the perforated-metal interior fittings of the box. Normally it requires to be cleaned about every 10,000 miles, except when riding is done in areas where the air is abnormally dusty. In this case it is desirable to clean the filter element about every 5000 miles.

To dismantle the filter, remove the front cover by unscrewing the centrally-positioned slotted nut. Then pull out with the fingers the filter element, wash it in petrol or paraffin, dip it in a light upper-cylinder lubricant such as Redex, drain off all surplus lubricant, and replace the element.

CHAPTER III

CORRECT LUBRICATION

WITHOUT correct (or perhaps it is more accurate to say "approximately correct") lubrication you cannot expect your Panther to retain for a long time its tune and youthfulness, and it will probably become prematurely aged. The author knows you do not want this to happen, and the best way to avoid it is to read carefully and put into practice the advice given in this chapter.

ENGINE LUBRICATION (1932-48)

Lubrication in a Nutshell. The fundamental idea at the bottom of all engine lubrication systems is to avoid friction and heat

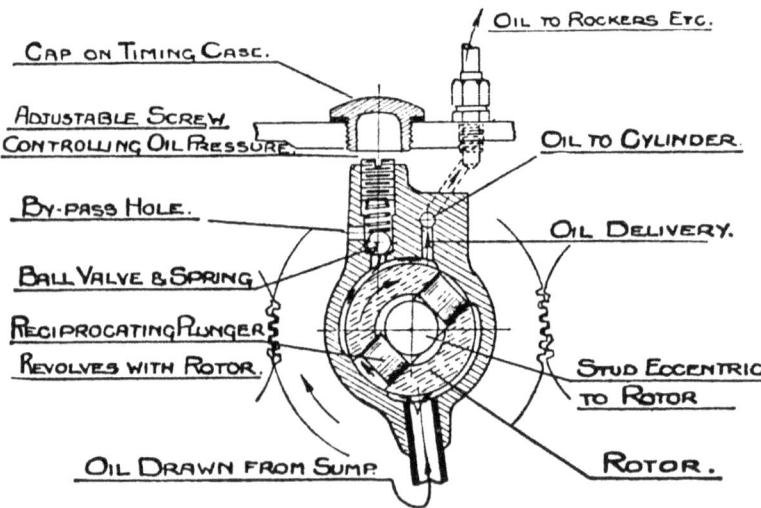

FIG. 9. SECTIONAL VIEW OF PANTHER PUMP (1936 TO 1948)
Earlier type pumps are illustrated opposite. The 1949-58 pump is shown on page 33

(which mean wear and tear) by maintaining between all contacting and moving surfaces an oil film which does (under a microscope) keep the surfaces actually apart to the extent of about 0·002 in. to about 0·008 in.

Every Panther expects that its owner will (a) use a good quality oil, (b) keep sufficient of it in circulation, (c) keep the oil free from pollution and dilution.

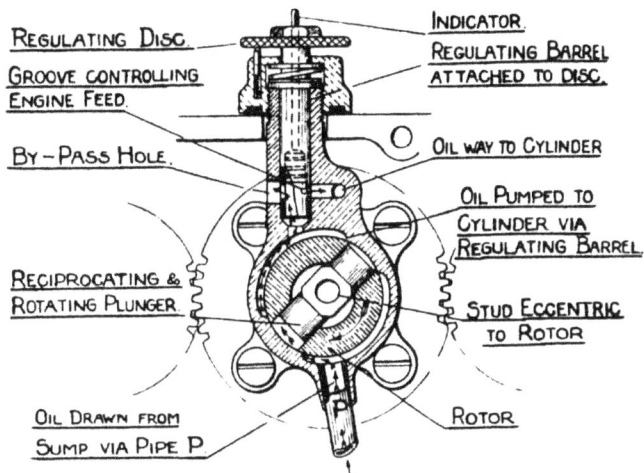

FIG. 10. SECTIONAL VIEW OF 1932-4 PANTHER OIL PUMP

On this pump an indicator is provided as shown above.
A view of the pump dismantled is shown in Fig. 12.
See also Fig. 22

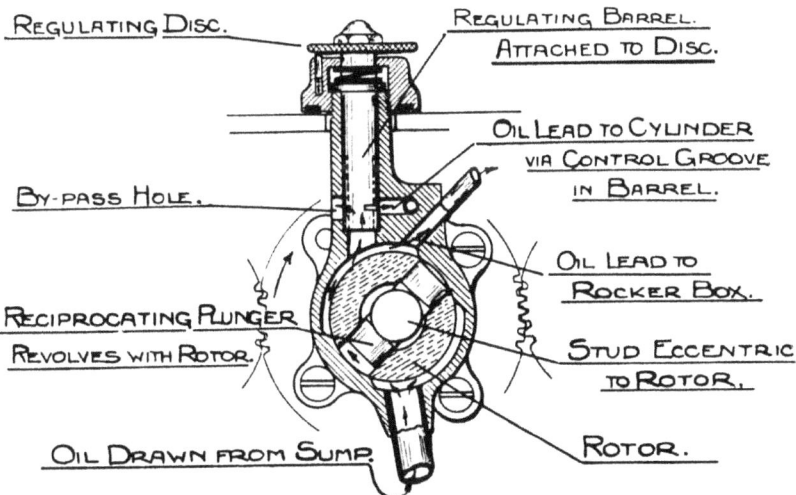

FIG. 11. SECTIONAL VIEW OF 1935 PANTHER PUMP

As the illustration shows, an indicator is omitted on this pump which is otherwise similar to that shown in Fig. 10. In the case of later pumps both the indicator and hand regulator are omitted, but an adjustable screw (Fig. 9) is provided to control the oil pressure

26 THE BOOK OF THE PANTHER (LIGHTWEIGHT)

The Panther Semi-wet Sump System (1932-48). This system has been used on *all* models. Up to the end of 1935 it had hand adjustment, but from 1936 onwards this has been omitted. A very small alteration in design distinguishes the two types as may be understood in a later paragraph. Oil from the sump reservoir (see Fig. 22) is drawn through a filter and suction pipe to a Panther oil pump which forces it at a pressure of roughly 10 lb. per sq. in. to a point at the rear of the cylinder wall, also to

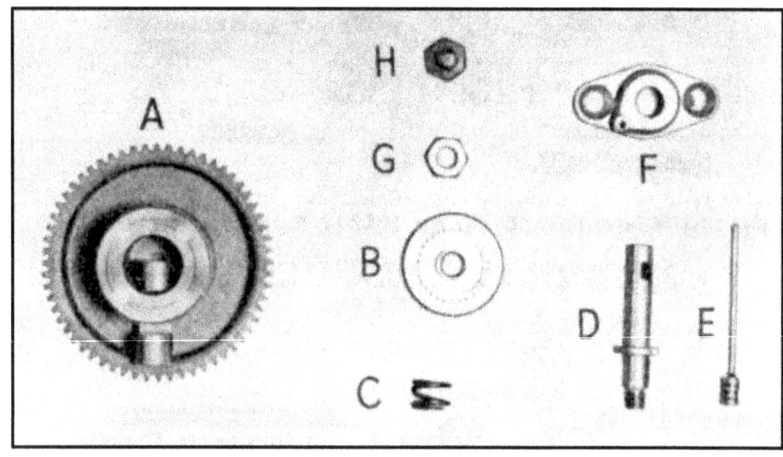

Fig. 12. The Oil Pump Dismantled (1932-5)

The position of the pump relative to the engine may be understood by reference to Fig. 22. The pump housing is not shown above but is illustrated in Figs. 10, 11, showing the complete unit assembled

A = Intermediate wheel with rotor and plunger (block omitted)
B = Regulating disc (1932-5)
C = Regulating spring
D = Regulating barrel (shown inverted)
E = Indicator rod (1932-4)
F = Flanged collar (1932-5)
G = Disc locknut
H = Barrel cap (1935 only)

the timing gear and in the case of post-1933 models to the rocker-box by an external pipe. Some of the oil supplied to the cylinder drops back on to the flywheels and crankshaft and splash lubricates the big-end, main bearings, etc., all surplus oil from both the timing case and crankcase being finally flung by the centrifugal force of the flywheels over a baffle into the oil reservoir, whence it is re-circulated as described. It is thus a constant circulation system with a certain amount of oil always in the engine sump beneath the flywheels. (See also pages 30, 31.)

The " Heart " of the System. This is a plunger oil pump which has no valves and may be understood by reference to Figs. 9 to 12. Fitted to the wall of the timing case is a flanged and circular body, hollowed out to receive the close-fitting rotor which forms

CORRECT LUBRICATION

the centre boss of the intermediate timing wheel (which rotates clockwise). The rotor itself (see Fig. 12) is also hollowed and on its boss circumference has two holes which act as bearings for a solid bronze plunger. Fitting over the recessed centre portion of this plunger, and at right angles to it, is a square-section block drilled to receive a stud fixed to the timing-case body eccentrically to the rotor. Thus, as the rotor revolves, a reciprocating motion is imparted to the pump plunger which thus constitutes a double-acting pump. As the plunger moves upwards in the rotor a vacuum is caused at the lower bearing hole, since the rotor fits closely in its housing. This vacuum occurs as the reciprocating plunger passes over a groove cut in the lower part of the housing. Oil is, therefore, sucked up from the sump reservoir via the filter and suction pipe, and fills up both the groove and the space vacated by the plunger. As the rotor further revolves, the end of the groove is passed, and the oil between the housing and the plunger is trapped. Having reached the limit of its upward stroke, the plunger commences to reverse its motion and in so doing expels the oil into a small opening cut in the top of the housing. This oil is then led to the cylinder and piston by the main oil-way, while some of it is by-passed to the timing gear, rocker-box as previously mentioned. A similar action is brought about alternately by each end of the plunger (see also page 32).

Regulation of Oil Supply (1932-5). Hand adjustment is provided on all 1932-5 models, but not on subsequent ones. Above the pump rotor housing, and integral with it, is a special housing containing the regulating barrel (*D*, Fig. 12), a cylindrical brass body having a groove cut at its lower end, adjacent to the main oil-way to the cylinder wall, in such a position that a slight rotation of it by means of the regulating disc enables the rider to vary the engine main oil supply. Below the knurled regulating disc (*B*, Fig. 12) is a flanged collar making an oil-tight joint with the crankcase to which it is screwed. The regulating disc, which is placed within reach of the saddle, can be rotated about a quarter of a revolution, the extreme positions (marked "Off," "On") being determined by two stops giving maximum and minimum oil delivery. On the grounds of safety, the regulating unit is designed so that the oil supply cannot be completely cut off.

Means of Checking Oil Circulation. On 1932-4 models it is possible to verify oil circulation by means of an automatic indicator. Passing through the regulating barrel and disc is a short indicator rod which is free to move up and down. The lower end of this rod (illustrated at *E*, Fig. 12) terminates in a small piston which (as is clearly shown in Fig. 10) is in contact with the main oil feed, and consequently under the normal working pressure of about 10 lb. per sq. in., it rises to its full extent and thereby provides a reliable and visible guide as to whether the oil pump is functioning properly.

On 1935 models although the regulator is retained, the indicator is omitted, a small cap (*H*, Fig. 12) screwing on to the top of the regulating barrel. On the 1936-48 models both the regulating disc and indicator are omitted, a flanged end-plate or cap being mounted over the original barrel housing which now has a spring-loaded ball valve, screw adjuster to control the oil pressure. If the oil pressure exceeds 20 lb. per sq. in., surplus oil is by-passed to the timing gear. On 1936-48 models minus indicator, to check oil circulation remove a small screw on the left-hand side of the crankcase, behind the cylinder. (See pages 30, 33.)

Beware of False Economy. To use an inferior oil or an unsuitable oil may theoretically seem economical, but in practice it is expensive! A worn piston, cylinder, big-end and main bearings are often attributable to false economy in this direction. All Panther owners are advised to replenish with one of the following engine oils: Castrol XXL (XL during winter), Shell X-100 40 (Shell X-100 30 during winter), Mobiloil BB (Mobiloil A during winter), B.P. Energol SAE 40 (SAE 30 during winter), Essolube 40 (Essolube 30 during winter). (See also pages 30 and 32.)

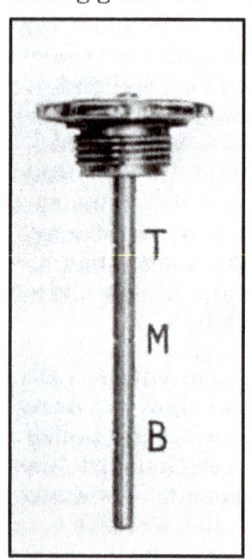

FIG. 13. REMOVE DIP-STICK EVERY 250 MILES
Keep the oil level on all models well above notch *M*. Never allow the level to fall below notch *B*

Keep the Oil Level High. The question of replenishment has already been touched on page 1, and suitable engine oils to use are given in the preceding paragraph. Here the author would stress the great importance of checking the oil level in the sump reservoir with the dip-stick about every 250 miles and topping up if necessary. In order to keep the oil as pure and cool as possible it is imperative not to allow the oil level to get too low. On the 1932-5 Panthers the filling orifice is placed on top of the timing case (Fig. 22) and the dip-stick lower down on the same side of the crankcase. When replenishing always remove the dip-stick to prevent the possibility of an air lock, and do not be over impatient; the oil takes an appreciable time to find the correct level as it has to flow through the duct in the timing case. On

CORRECT LUBRICATION

post-1935 models the dip-stick and filler cap are combined (see Fig. 13) and are situated forward on the near side of the crankcase so as to prevent excessive filling by careless riders (which might cause the oil level to rise above the sump baffle).

On 1932-5 models do not fill above the top notch T (Fig. 13), on the dip-stick, and be sure that the level never drops below notch B. To obtain the best results, the author would advise the reader to maintain the oil level between notches M, T. On all models fill *slightly below* notch T if the engine smokes.

To Check Oil Circulation. On models prior to 1935 a glance at the indicator (Fig. 10) will tell you whether the oil pump is doing its duty properly. If it is, you will notice that the indicator rod is protruded (see page 27). Should the indicator fail to rise when the engine is running, it would denote that the filter is choked, the suction pipe damaged, or the pump itself is at fault.

To check oil circulation on 1934-48 models it is necessary to remove the small screw on the near side of the crankcase at the rear of the cylinder and observe whether oil issues in quantity with the engine running. On models without an adjustment of the pump, checking the oil circulation is seldom called for, as the lubrication system is practically foolproof and very reliable, if the filter is kept clean. 1949-58 engines: (see page 33).

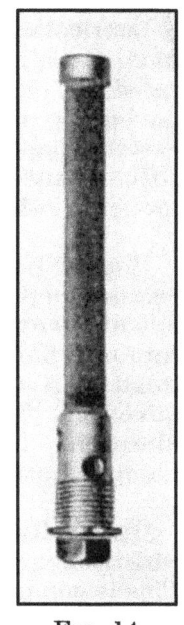

FIG. 14
THE GAUZE
SUMP FILTER

For position in engine, see Fig. 22

Correct Lubrication. As regards the quantity of oil supplied by the pump to the cylinder and rocker-box, this is on models later than 1935 entirely automatic as already explained, and provides correct lubrication for all throttle openings. On 1932-5 models with hand regulation some discretion must be used in arriving at the best pump adjustment. During the running-in period (see page 9) the oil supply should be on the liberal side and the regulator disc should be turned towards the "on" position until a *thin blue haze* is visible at the exhaust; but do not permit the engine actually to "smoke." After the running-in period cut down the supply gradually until a blue haze is emitted only when accelerating from a standstill. For ordinary touring on give and take roads, turn on the regulator disc about three to four notches and be careful never to force it beyond the stops or to run with it turned right off. For hard driving, increase the supply accordingly by turning the disc to the full "on" position (see page 27).

Clean Sump Filter Every 1000 miles (1932-48). After the first 500 miles and subsequently every 1000 miles the gauze filter in the sump (Fig. 14) should be removed by unscrewing the plated hexagon nut on the bottom right-hand side of the sump, just below the timing case. Before doing this, however, put a suitable receptacle beneath it to avoid an unholy mess on the floor when the oil runs out. It is best to drain the sump when the engine is *warm* as this facilitates thorough draining. After removing the filter, clean the gauze thoroughly in petrol and see that the base holes are clear. Beware cleaning the gauze with a fluffy rag for obvious reasons. After refitting the filter replenish the oil sump with suitable engine oil (see also pages 28 and 32).

Lubrication of Rocker-box and Valve Guides. On 1932-3 models the rocker-box and valve guides are automatically lubricated by oil mist thrown up the push-rod cover, and on later models by oil fed direct to the rocker-box from the pump by an external pipe, and no attention on the part of the rider is necessary. After adjusting the tappets, make sure that the cover beds down properly, otherwise oil leakage may occur.

Engine Lubrication (**1936 to 1948**). If a P. & M. Panther engine tends to "smoke," it should be noted that the supply of oil to the cylinder can be reduced by removing the small metal cap on top of the timing case and turning with a screwdriver the small slotted screw exposed very slightly in an *anti-clockwise* direction. To increase the oil supply, turn the screw in a *clockwise* direction. It is not, however, desirable to alter the original pump adjustment unless essential.

During Running-in. It is beneficial to mix Colloidal Graphite with the engine oil in the proportion of 1 pint to 1 gallon of oil. This is conducive to cool running and protects the bearings from metal pick-up. The above advice applies only to a few 1932 type engines.

On 1938 Models. The semi-wet sump system is the same as on previous models (see page 26) but the drainage of oil from the rocker-box has improvements, the oil returning to the sump via a channel formed in the cylinder wall. Also an air-release valve (Fig. 15) is incorporated in the engine-sprocket nut. See also opposite.

On 1939 and 1945-8 Models. The semi-wet sump system with Panther oil pump (see page 26) is unchanged, but the 1938 method of draining oil from the rocker-box (channel) has been

CORRECT LUBRICATION

abandoned in favour of an external oil pipe between the cylinder head and sump on the near side. This, together with the fitting of a copper cylinder-head gasket, reduces the risk of oil leakage.

As during 1938, an air-release valve is fitted on the drilled driving-side mainshaft and is integral with the engine sprocket nut (see Fig. 15). No spring is used, the valve being in the form of a light disc. Previous to 1938 a crankcase air-release valve was provided, but this was rather unsatisfactory, excessive lubrication and wastage of oil having been experienced by a number of riders. Owners of 1936-7 models troubled with over-oiling are advised to obtain one of the latest engine sprocket nuts which can be fitted in place of the existing nut. Fitting takes only a few minutes. On pre-1936 engines, however, the 1938 type valve cannot be fitted to the engine mainshaft.

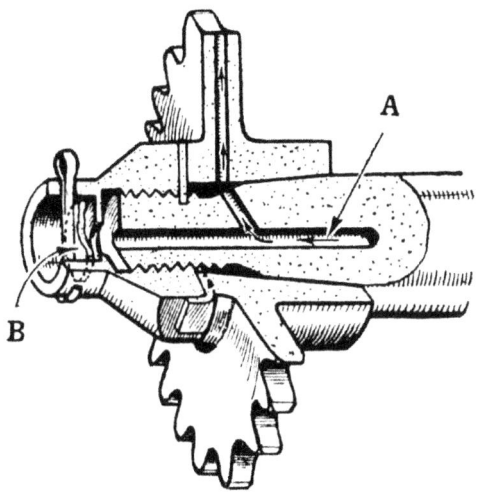

FIG. 15. SHOWING METHOD OF LUBRICATING THE PRIMARY CHAIN, AND THE AIR-RELEASE VALVE

On the 1939 to 1948 models, oil (*A*) reaches the primary chain in the manner indicated. At *B* is shown the air-release valve disc, integral with the engine sprocket nut on 1938 and later models. (See also page 34)

(*By Courtesy of "The Motor Cycle," London*)

"Maglita" and Dynamo Lubrication. On "Maglita" models place a spot of oil on the steel cam and a drop of oil in the holes under the contact-breaker and in the lubricator at the driving end about once every 1000 miles. On coil-ignition models the Miller dynamo bearings are packed with grease on assembly and this should suffice for 10,000-15,000 miles; the dynamo should then be returned to the makers to have the bearings repacked with H.M.P. grease. Smear a little petroleum jelly on the contact-breaker cam every 5000 miles. (See page 34.)

ENGINE LUBRICATION (1949-1958)

The 1949 Lubrication System. The semi-wet sump lubrication system provided on 1949 and later Panthers is fundamentally similar to the earlier system described on page 26 and the pump, the "heart" of the system, is little altered. The system used on the redesigned Panther engines does, however, include some modifications.

Oil is drawn from the Panther pump (see Fig. 17) from the sump which is integral with the crankcase. The pump then pressure feeds the oil to the working parts as indicated in Fig. 16.

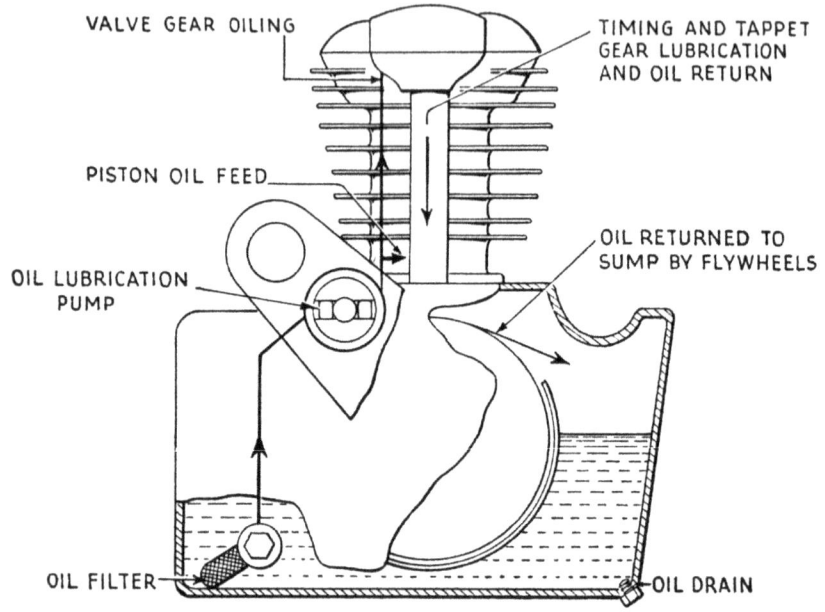

Fig. 16. Diagram of Oil Circulation System (1949 Onwards)

Oil is fed to the rear of the cylinder wall, the driving-side main bearing, the timing-side main bearing, and the rocker-box.

After circulation the oil is returned to the sump automatically by means of the flywheels, and the drainage from the overhead valve gear helps to lubricate the timing gears, which operate in an oil-bath (the timing chest being kept about half full).

Care of Lubrication System. Beware of false economy in regard to engine oil and always use a good brand of the correct grade (see page 28).

Keep the oil level high (see pages 28-29) and check the oil level with the dip-stick every 250 miles. Top-up as required. Clean the sump filter and change the oil every 2000 miles (see later paragraphs).

Oil Replenishment. It is vitally important always to refill with the correct grade and make of oil. The five brands recommended are all equally suitable, but it is a good plan not to mix

CORRECT LUBRICATION

them. Always top-up with the same brand and grade as is already in use.

Never buy "loose" oil, as its lubricating qualities may be poor and it may cause untold damage.

To Check Oil Circulation. The 1949 and later oil circulation system, like its predecessors, is almost foolproof, provided the filter is kept clean and the oil reservoir is regularly topped-up to the top notch on the dip-stick.

If no trace of a blue haze is visible at the exhaust on accelerating the engine sharply, it is advisable to check the oil circulation. To

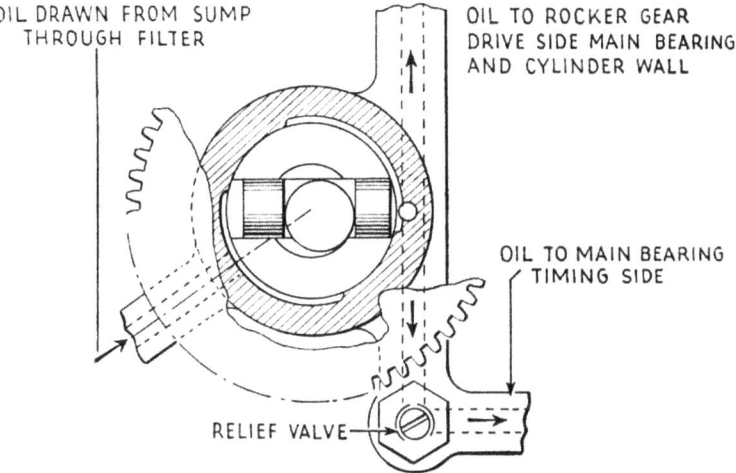

Fig. 17. Partly Sectioned View of Panther Oil Pump (1949 Onwards)
For position of pump on engine, see Fig. 16

do this, slacken the union nut at the base of the oil feed pipe to the rocker-box and note whether any oil emerges. No oil pump or oil pressure adjustment (pre-set) is provided.

Clean Filter and Change Oil Every 2000 Miles. In the case of the redesigned Panther engines it is advisable every 2000 miles (also after the first 500 miles) to remove the filter, drain the sump, and replenish with fresh oil (page 28).

The oil filter (Fig. 52) is situated at the rear bottom corner of the timing case side of the sump, and below the gauze (screwed up into the bottom of the sump) is the drain plug. A second drain plug is provided at the forward end of the sump (see Fig. 16), and this plug should also be removed. There is a tendency for oil to collect at the front end, ahead of the internal baffle.

To facilitate thorough draining of the sump, you should drain the oil off after a run when the oil is *hot*. Remove both the filter and the screwed drain plug. Be most careful not to lose or damage the filter washer. Clean the filter thoroughly in petrol and replace it. Then screw the drain plugs home and replenish the oil reservoir to just below the top notch on the dip-stick. It is not advisable to replenish right up to the top notch, as this tends to cause some over-lubrication.

Failure of Crankcase Release Valve. The crankcase release valve (referred to on page 31) prevents the building-up of excessive pressure inside the crankcase. Its failure to function properly may convey to the uninitiated the impression that the rotary oil pump is forcing too much oil into the engine.

If, therefore, the engine tends to smoke and some oil leakage develops, make sure that the release valve is not sticking or dirt preventing its seating properly. It is advisable to renew the valve disc after a considerable mileage, as some wear inevitably occurs.

In the case of the 1938-49 and later type crankcase release valve (integral with the engine-sprocket nut), remove the nut and clean it thoroughly in petrol. See that all dirt, gumminess, etc., is eliminated. Shake the nut vigorously; the disc should be quite free to rattle. To remove the disc, tap out the pin which retains it.

As mentioned on page 31, the 1936-7 type release valve should be replaced by the 1938 and later type if over-lubrication persists in spite of unscrewing it from the engine-sprocket retaining nut and cleaning the valve. On replacing this type of valve, apply a *very* small amount of grease to the disc. This will retain the disc to the centre pin while you screw the valve home, and thereby prevent the disc being damaged or trapped.

Lubrication of Lucas Magneto (Model 75). On the 1949 and later 350 c.c. Model 75 the ball bearings of the Lucas magneto armature-shaft are packed with grease during assembly by the makers and no oiling is required. After a very big mileage it is advisable to return the magneto to a Lucas service depot for thorough overhaul and re-greasing of the bearings.

Every 5000 miles smear a little petroleum jelly on the cam. Be most careful not to allow any to get on the contacts. At the same time push aside the locating spring (see Fig. 47), prise the rocker arm off its bearing, and lightly smear some petroleum jelly on the pivot.

The Lucas Contact-breaker (Model 65). Very little attention is needed. About every 5000 miles smear a little petroleum jelly

CORRECT LUBRICATION

on the cam, taking great care not to allow any to get on the contacts. Also lubricate the rocker arm pivot similarly.

Lubrication of Lucas Dynamo. Both bearings are packed with grease by the makers. Further lubrication is not required until the dynamo is returned to the makers and stripped down for inspection and overhaul or replaced by a "factory-exchange" unit.

MOTOR-CYCLE LUBRICATION (1932-58)

Burman Gearbox (Pre-1949). New Burman gearboxes are charged with sufficient lubricant for at least 1000 miles running without any attention. But at the end of this period and subsequently every 1000 miles the metal plate on top of the gearbox should be removed by undoing the two nuts, and 2-3 oz. of Wakefield Castrolease Medium, B.P. Energrease AO, Vacuum Mobilgrease No. 2, Shell Retinax A or CD, or Esso Grease should be injected into the gearbox. Do not fill the gearbox completely. It is designed to run about *one-third full*, and this is quite sufficient for proper lubrication. Turning the rear wheel over will facilitate filling, and when replenishing the gearbox do not forget to grease the kick-starter and foot gear-change mechanism.

Sturmey-Archer Gearbox Lubrication. This type of gearbox fitted on many 1932-3 Red Panthers requires lubrication at the same period as the Burman gearbox. Every 1000 miles a small quantity of light lubricant, e.g., Castrol Grand Prix, should be injected into the gearbox filler orifice. Occasionally verify the level of lubricant in the gearbox, which should be from *one-third to half full*. If the period recommended above for gearbox lubrication does not maintain this level, reduce the period accordingly.

Burman Gearbox (1949 Onwards). All new three- and four-speed Burman gearboxes are filled with sufficient lubricant for 1000 miles running. Grease (see page 37) or *summer-grade* engine oil (see page 28)* is advised for three- or four-speed gearboxes respectively. Every 1500 miles replenish the gearbox with 2-3 oz. of grease or engine oil through the filler plug or the slotted cap on three- or four-speed gearboxes respectively. Also (where grease nipples are provided), grease the kick-starter and foot gear-change mechanism on three-speed gearboxes. On all four-speed gearboxes a separate oil-level plug is provided immediately to the rear of the kick-starter crank, and it is impossibe to over-fill the gearbox when the plug is removed.

* When Esso is concerned, use Essolube 50, not 40.

In the case of Burman four-speed gearboxes lubricated by engine oil, it is advisable about every 5000 miles to drain the gearbox completely, flush it out with suitable flushing oil, and then replenish it with about one pint of summer-grade engine oil to the level of the filler plug orifice. The screwed drain plug is located low down at the rear of the gearbox casing. Before replenishing the gearbox with new oil, make sure that the drain plug and washer are replaced, and tighten the drain plug firmly. As soon as oil begins to trickle from the level-plug orifice, replace the level-plug and filler cap. Be careful to tighten the former securely.

Replenish Oil-bath Chain Case Where Fitted. On all 1938–58 Panther lightweight models the primary chain runs completely enclosed in an oil-bath chain case and is (pre-1949) lubricated by a pipe leading from the engine breather. It is desirable, however, in order to ensure thorough lubrication of the fast moving primary chain to remove the chain-case inspection cap every 500 miles and replenish the chain case with the appropriate type of engine oil. The separate level-plug determines the correct oil level and oil should be poured in until it commences to trickle out through the plug orifice. Obviously it is impossible to overfill the chain case. No separate plug is fitted on 1939 Model 40 and later models. Replenish with sufficient lubricant to ensure that the bottom run of the chain dips into it during its rotation. Drain and refill every 5000 miles.

—Where Not Fitted. Where no oil-bath is fitted, lubrication is then automatic (from the crankcase), but it is desirable to remove the chain every 2000 miles, clean it in paraffin and grease as described in the next paragraph.

Secondary Chain Lubrication. On all models the secondary chain requires to be smeared with grease. To be on the safe side, grease little and often. About once every 2000 miles in the summer and more frequently in the winter it is a good plan to remove the secondary chain and immerse it in a paraffin bath, allowing it to soak thoroughly so as to remove all traces of dirt. After being carefully wiped the chain should, before being refitted, be immersed in a bath of molten tallow, or as a poorer substitute engine oil and grease. If the latter method is used the chain should be allowed to soak overnight so as to ensure that the oil penetrates all the link joints.

Grease Fork Spindles Every 500 miles. About every 500 miles apply the grease gun to the (1032–46) front-forks nipples until

CORRECT LUBRICATION

grease begins to exude from the spindle ends. Suitable greases for grease gun lubrication of the fork-spindle nipples and all other nipples on 1932-55 Panthers are given below.

Lubrication of Telescopic Front Forks (1947-55). The advice given for the pre-1947 girder-type front forks do not, of course, apply to the 1947-52 Panther-Dowty "Oleomatic" type forks. With these forks apply the grease gun every 500 miles to the nipple (shown at 8 in Fig. 18) provided for lubricating the bottom bearing of each fork leg. Fork leg replenishment is dealt with on page 80.

1953 and subsequent rigid and spring frame 250 c.c. and 350 c.c. Panthers are fitted with Panther-type telescopic front forks. These have no grease nipples provided (other than those for steering head lubrication). New forks are filled with sufficient engine oil (half a pint, SAE 40) for thousands of miles. After covering about 5000 miles it may be necessary (if initial stiffness persists) to drain and replenish both fork legs. The appropriate instructions for doing this are given on page 102. (See also page 40.)

Suitable Greases. Suitable greases for lubricating the 1932-46 front forks, the secondary chain, and the various motor-cycle parts requiring grease gun lubrication are—

1. Wakefield's Castrolease CL. (Medium: three-speed gearbox.)
2. Esso Grease.
3. Shell Retinax A or CD.
4. Vacuum Mobilgrease No. 2.
5. B.P. Energrease AO.

Grease Steering Head Bearings Every 3000 Miles. To prevent stiffness of steering and possibly damage to the ball bearings, grease the steering-head bearings lightly about every 3000 miles.

Oil Handlebar Controls Weekly. Apply a few spots of oil weekly to the handlebar control levers, exposed nipples, and exposed ends (both ends) of the control cables. Do not overlook the rear-brake linkage, the link for the front-brake operating arm, and the exposed end of the exhaust-valve lifter cable at the cable adjuster near the petrol tank nose.

The Speedometer Gearbox. To prevent undue wear and to ensure speedometer reliability, it is advisable to disconnect the flexible drive about every 3000 miles and grease the speedometer gearbox with one of the greases previously mentioned.

38 THE BOOK OF THE PANTHER (LIGHTWEIGHT)

Oil the Wheel Hubs. Cup-and-cone type ball bearings are fitted to the hubs of most 1932-9 Red Panthers, and journal-type ball bearings to the hubs of 1938-58 P. & M. Panther lightweights. Neither type of bearing should be greased. Instead, oil both hubs, using engine oil, about every 1000 miles. Avoid excessive lubrication, otherwise some oil may reach the brake shoes and adversely affect braking efficiency.

The Brake Cam Spindles. An oil hole covered by a spring clip is provided for the lubrication of each spindle. Every 1000 miles insert a few drops of oil.

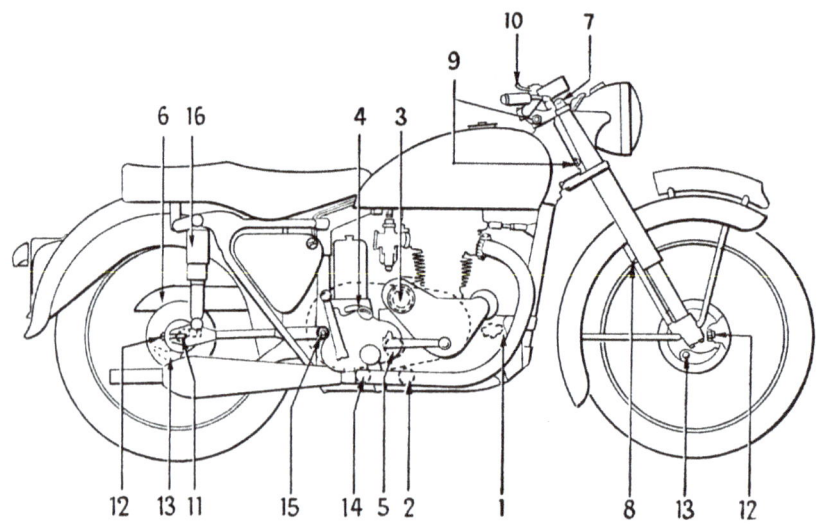

FIG. 18. LUBRICATION CHART FOR 1949-58 PANTHER MODELS 65 AND 75

A Model 75 Panther with rear suspension shown in outline. Point No. 8 applies only to 1947-52 models with Panther-Dowty "Oleomatic" front forks; where these forks are specified, point No. 9 does not include a grease nipple for the steering head *upper* bearing. On rigid-frame models points 15 and 16 do not apply

The Rear-brake Pedal. A grease nipple is provided for lubricating the pedal shaft. Every 500 miles apply the grease gun. Occasionally apply a few spots of thin oil to the plunger of the stop-light switch.

Rear Suspension. Grease the "swinging arm" pivots every 500 miles. The Panther-type rear-suspension units (fitted to 1953 models) are initially filled with sufficient engine oil (38 c.c., SAE 40) for many thousands of miles, but after covering 500 miles it may be necessary to insert some additional engine oil if the

KEY TO FIG. 18

Point	Description	Lubrication, etc. Required	See Page
1	Sump reservoir	Every 250 miles check oil level and top-up.	1, 28
2	Sump filter	Every 2000 miles change oil and clean filter.	33
3	Contact-breaker { magneto (75)	Every 5000 miles smear a little petroleum jelly on the cam and the rocker arm pivot.	34
	coil (65)	As for mag. contact-breaker.	34
4	Burman gearbox { 3-speed	Every 1500 miles replenish with 2-3 oz. of grease. Also grease kick-starter and foot gear-change mechanism (if nipples provided).	35
	4-speed	Every 1500 miles replenish with 2-3 oz. of summer grade engine oil to level of filler plug orifice. Every 5000 miles drain gearbox, flush out, and replenish with new oil.	35
5	Primary chain	Every 500 miles replenish oil-bath chain case with the appropriate type of engine oil. Drain and refill every 5000 miles.	36
6	Secondary chain	Grease regularly. Every 2000 miles remove, clean, and grease.	36
7, 8	Front forks { 1947-52 Dowty "Oleomatic"	Every 500 miles grease nipple at point 8. If forks "bottom" when correctly inflated, top-up.	80
	1953-8 Panther	If stiffness persists after 5000 miles, drain and replenish.	102
9	Steering head	Every 3000 miles grease lower bearing (1947-52), or both bearings (1953-8).	37
10	Handlebar controls	Weekly apply a few spots of oil to control levers, exposed nipples, and cables.	37
11	Speedometer gearbox	Every 3000 miles grease.	37
12	Wheel hubs	Every 1000 miles inject a small amount of engine oil.	38
13	Brake cam spindles	Every 1000 miles apply a few drops of oil.	38
14	Rear-brake pedal	Weekly grease the nipple.	38
15	"Swinging arm" pivots	Grease every 500 miles.	38
16	Rear Susp'n. { Panther unit	If too free after 500 miles, top-up with engine oil.	38
	Armstrong	No lubrication required.	40

suspension units develop too free an action. Instructions for topping-up are given on page 105. In the event of the suspension unit action being too stiff, drain off a little oil.

The Armstrong-type units (fitted to 1954 and later Panthers) contain sufficient SAE 10 mineral oil for an indefinite running period, and no maintenance is necessary.

Lubrication of Stands. It is important to grease occasionally the pivots of centre and prop stands.

The 1956-8 Panther Telescopic Front Forks. These front forks are, except for slight modifications, identical to the 1947-55 type. Referring to Fig. 55, the gland housing (7) has been modified to an aluminium housing which also forms a shroud protruding from the bottom of the outer cover-tube. In addition, the large-diameter coil spring on the outside of the centre tube (13) has been replaced by a smaller-diameter spring, placed inside the centre tube, locating on a peg fixed in the fork-end lug.

The maintenance and dismantling instructions given on page 102 are applicable to the modified 1956-8 front forks, but carefully note the following points. *The correct amount of engine oil required for each fork leg is one-quarter of a pint.* The main oil seal (good for thousands of miles) need not be disturbed unless a serious oil leakage develops. A dust-excluding ring (made of hard synthetic rubber) is interposed between the aluminium housing (7) and the inside of the bottom tube (12). Should this ring eventually become dry or damp, stiffness or a slight squeak respectively is likely to develop, and the remedy in either case is to squirt a little oil through the small hole facing forward near the base of the bottom tube.

CHAPTER IV

IN THE GARAGE

IN this chapter it is proposed to deal with various important maintenance and overhauling matters other than carburettor tuning and lubrication which have been fully discussed in the preceding two chapters. Panther maintenance is really very simple, provided you work methodically and have just a little "mechanical sense." It includes a number of simple

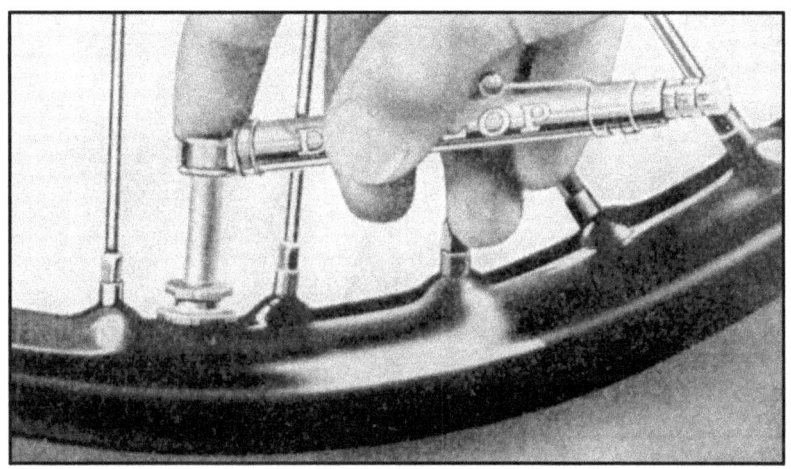

FIG. 19. AN ITEM YOU MUST HAVE

Tyre pressures should be checked frequently with a Schrader No. 7750, a Holdtite, a Romac, or a Dunlop pencil-type No. 6 gauge, and adjusted if necessary

(*Dunlop Rubber Co. Ltd.*)

adjustments, decarbonizing, and general overhaul. These matters will be dealt with in this order.

Useful Items for the Garage. In addition to rigging up a work bench and vice if possible, it is very desirable to obtain a number of items which for the benefit of the novice the author will describe. As regards tools, in addition to the tool kit on your machine (dealt with in a later paragraph), you will require a good set of tyre **levers, a** fairly large screwdriver (for decarbonizing), a valve-spring compressor (see page 62), a feeler gauge (for checking plug gaps), a pressure gauge for checking tyre pressures (Fig. 19), and a gudgeon-pin extractor (see page 95). All these items can if desired be purchased from accessory dealers (see page 83).

It is also a good plan, if you mean "real business," to invest in a soldering outfit (for mending broken cables), a chain rivet extractor, a large pair of pliers, a steel rule, a half round file, a centre punch and a moderately light hammer. Other *necessary* items will include some emery cloth, some valve grinding paste (coarse and

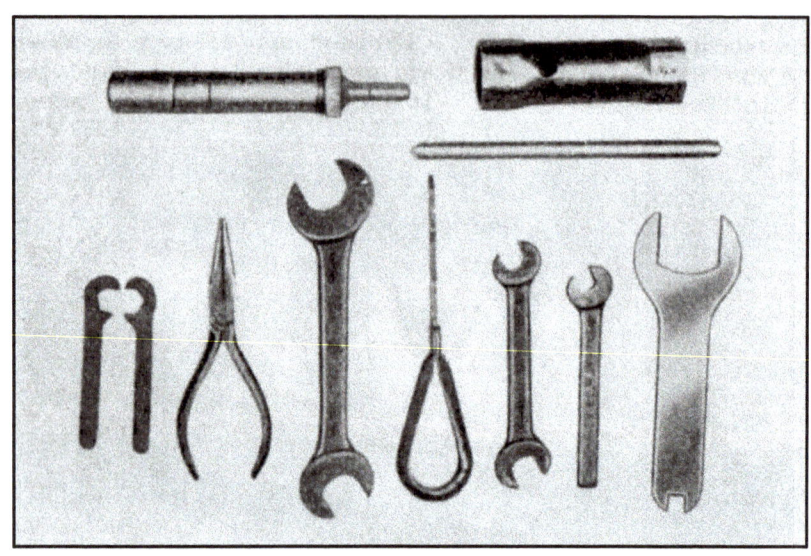

FIG. 20. THE RED PANTHER TOOL KIT

The tools shown at the bottom from left to right are: small spanners for tappet adjustment (not required on 1935 engines); pliers for gudgeon-pin circlip removal; $\frac{7}{16}$ in., $\frac{3}{8}$ in. spanner for gearbox and axle nuts, Model 20, (top end) and front fork bottom spindle (bottom end); screwdriver; $\frac{3}{16}$ in., $\frac{1}{4}$ in. spanner for engine nuts and various cycle parts; $\frac{3}{8}$ in. spanner for front fork top spindle nuts; spanner for steering head nut (top end) and gearbox eccentric adjustment (bottom end). Above these tools are shown (left) the grease gun and (right) a $\frac{9}{16}$ in., $\frac{1}{2}$ in. box spanner and tommy-bar for the sparking plug and axle nuts, Models 30, 70. The contact-breaker spanner (with feeler gauge) and $\frac{5}{16}$ in. box spanner for cylinder head nuts are not shown

fine), a suction-type valve grinding tool, a battery filler, a tyre **repair outfit**, a tin of engine oil (page 28), a tin of grease (page 37), **a can** of paraffin, plenty of rags (of the non-fluffy sort), a stiff bristle brush for scouring mud off the crankcase, a small wire brush for the plug, a pail, a couple of sponges, a chamois leather, polishing cloths, and a tin of enamel polish. You will also need some enamelled dishes and jars for washing parts in, a large driptray, etc. Cleanliness in the garage is nearly as important as

IN THE GARAGE

keeping the machine clean. If a habit is formed of letting the machine go dirty, defects will go unnoticed, rust will probably set in, performance may decline and quick depreciation will occur. If the garage floor is allowed to become soaked in paraffin or oil, the tyres will inevitably pick it up and will rot badly, quite apart from the question of ruining drawing-room carpets! One final tip—

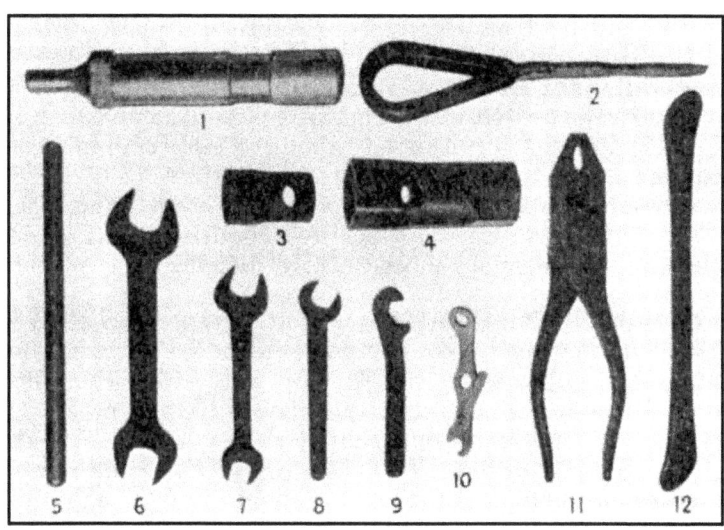

Fig. 21. The Panther Tool Kit (Models 65, 75)

1. Tecalemit grease-gun
2. All-metal screwdriver
3. Box spanner for gearbox pivot-mounting bolts
4. Double-ended box spanner for sparking plug and wheel spindle nuts
5. Tommy bar
6. Double-ended general purpose spanner ($\frac{5}{16}$ in., $\frac{1}{4}$ in. W.)
7. Double-ended tappet head locknut and general purpose spanner ($\frac{3}{16}$ in., $\frac{1}{8}$ in. W.)
8. Spanner for rocker-box oil-feed pipe nuts ($\frac{3}{8}$ in. A.F.)
9. Spanner for tappet head adjustment
10. Contact-breaker spanner with 0·012 in. feeler gauge
11. Cutting-pliers
12. Tyre lever

Get hold of a tin of really good hand cleanser. You will certainly need it, especially on Sunday just before lunch!

Take a Look at the Tool Kit. If you have never tackled any dismantling or adjustments on your Panther, take a good look at the tool kit, similar to the tools illustrated and explained in Figs. 20-21. These tools will be found adequate for most maintenance jobs. A convenient tool, however, in addition to these and the items suggested in a previous paragraph is an adjustable spanner. In the author's opinion you cannot do better than obtain a Lucas girder wrench.

44 THE BOOK OF THE PANTHER (LIGHTWEIGHT)

SOME SIMPLE ADJUSTMENTS

Why Valve Clearances are Important. The exhaust valve often operates at a temperature as high as 700° centigrade, and if it fails to close completely during the firing stroke there is a grave risk of the hot gases damaging its ground seating surface. Loss of compression will also occur, and the power output of the engine will markedly decline if there is insufficient clearance for either the inlet or exhaust valve. Excessive clearances, on the other hand, cause irritating valve clatter, subject the valves to undue stresses and generally mar engine efficiency. In other words, it is exceedingly important to maintain the valve clearances correct at all times. Adjustment is not often called for except in the case of a new engine where the valves tend to bed down for a time. Owners of new machines are therefore advised to check the clearances every few hundred miles. After decarbonizing and grinding-in the valves the clearances should always be checked.

The Panther Valve Clearances. In the case of all 1932 models onwards *with the engine cold* there should be *no clearance* between the hardened valve stem end-cap or valve and the actuating rocker pad or adjusting screw (fitted on 1932-4 models). This applies to both the inlet and exhaust valves. When checking the clearances the piston must be at the top of the firing stroke, and the adjustment on all 1932-4 models should be such that although there is no clearance perceptible on attempting to "shake" the rocker up and down with the fingers, the adjuster screw exerts no actual pressure on the valve or end-cap. They must just be in actual contact—nothing more. In the case of 1935, and later models, where making an adjustment entails removing the rocker-box end plate or telescoping the push-rod cover respectively, the best method of arriving at the correct adjustment is to adjust as described below until the push-rods are free to revolve but have *no vertical* play.

To Adjust Clearances (1932-4 Models). The means of adjustment is illustrated in Fig. 22 (also *E*, Fig. 34). With the small spanners provided in the tool kit loosen the locknut and then turn the hexagon-headed screw until the above setting is obtained. Be careful to check the clearance after tightening the locknut.

To Adjust Clearances (1935 Models). On 1935 models an eccentric adjustment of the rocker shafts is provided (see Fig. 23). First of all remove the rocker-box end plate and then pull the exhaust-valve lifter off its stud. The Bowden cable itself need not be disconnected. Next slacken both rocker shaft locknuts which are situated on the sparking plug side of the cylinder head and

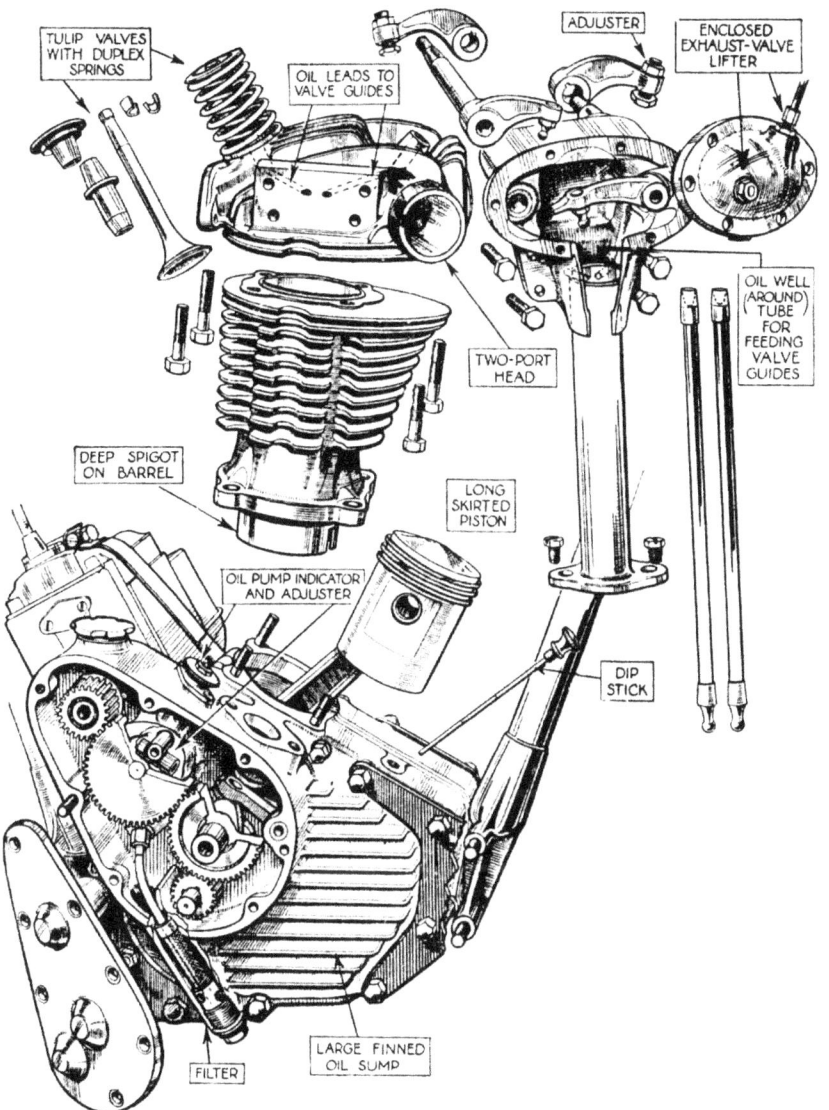

FIG. 22. SHOWING VALVE CLEARANCE ADJUSTMENT AND OTHER DETAILS OF 1932-4 RED PANTHER ENGINE ("MAGLITA")

Since 1934 adjuster screws on the O.H. rockers have been omitted, the valve actuating pads being integral with the rockers. During 1935 an eccentric spindle adjustment (Fig. 23) was used and after 1935 adjustable tappets with telescopic push-rod cover (Fig. 24) have been provided. Other alterations made to the engine since 1933 include an improved rocker-box cast integral with the cylinder head, positive lubrication of the rocker-box by an external oil pipe, and a combined dip-stick and filler cap. Fig. 52 shows an exploded view of the 1949–53 engine

(*By Courtesy of "The Motor Cycle," London*)

revolve each rocker shaft by means of a screwdriver inserted in the slot provided until the correct valve clearance is obtained. To decrease the clearance, rotate the inlet rocker shaft *anti-clockwise* and the exhaust rocker shaft *clockwise*. The maximum adjustment is one half turn which is equivalent to ⅛ in. adjustment at the rocker arm. It is important to retighten the locknuts

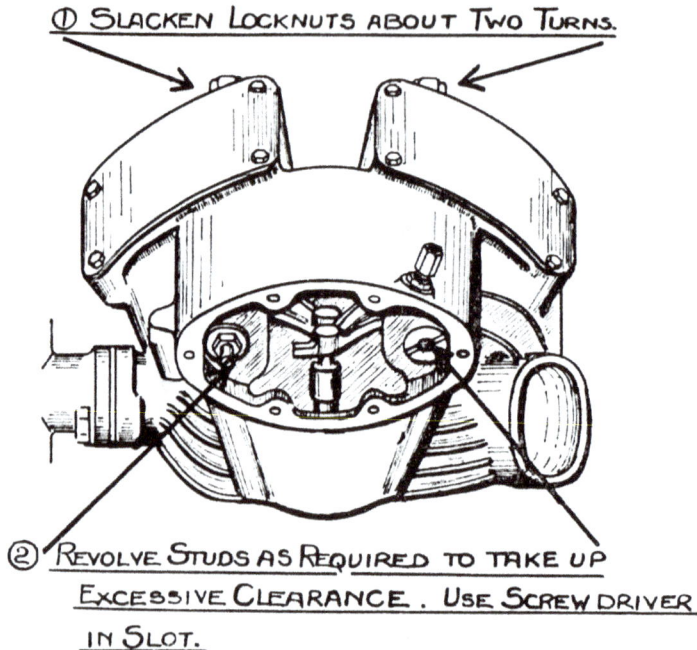

Fig. 23. Valve Clearance Adjustment on 1935 Engines
Make the eccentric adjustment in the order 1, 2, 3

while holding the rocker shafts with the screwdriver. Afterwards check the adjustment carefully.

To Adjust Clearances (1936 Onwards). Models built since 1935 have an ordinary tappet adjustment similar to that on the heavyweight 600 c.c. models. To expose the tappets and push-rods unscrew the push-rod cover tube hexagon-headed screws at its base and telescope the tube upwards. Then with the tappet spanners unscrew the locknut (Fig. 24) and adjust the cupped tappet head (on which the push-rod rests) until the correct clearance is obtained. Finally retighten the locknut and again check the adjustment (see page 44). See that valves are shut.

IN THE GARAGE

Is There Any Backlash at the Exhaust-valve Lifter? Before checking the valve clearance and at all other times it is very important always to allow a little backlash ($\frac{1}{16}$ in. to $\frac{1}{8}$ in.) at the exhaust-valve lifter lever on the handlebars, with the exhaust valve fully closed, otherwise the exhaust valve may find it impossible to seat properly with the result that loss of compression, power, banging in the silencer and a hot exhaust pipe may result. An adjustment for the Bowden cable stop is provided on one side of the rocker-box or (on 1949-58 models) just in front of the petrol-tank nose. Before attempting an adjustment, however, loosen the locknut, and afterwards make certain that it is re-tightened securely.

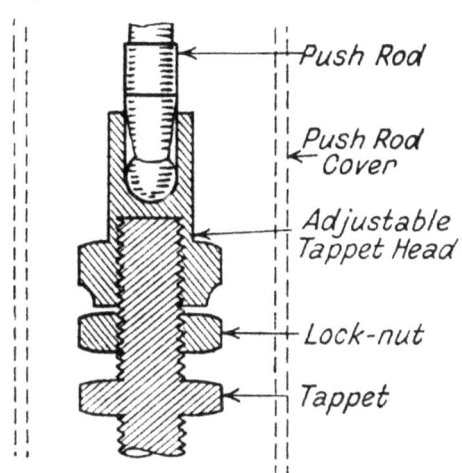

Fig. 24. Tappet Adjustment (1936 onwards)

Keep the Plug Gap Correct. It is fairly safe to say that the majority of engine troubles, and especially difficult starting and misfiring, is due to a dirty or otherwise defective sparking plug. Even the most expensive plug is not absolutely proof against the terrific heat of combustion, and the electrode points gradually burn away with the result that the gap between them becomes gradually enlarged. It is therefore advisable every 2000-3000 miles, or whenever engine trouble develops, to remove the plug and check the gap at the electrodes with a feeler gauge, and if necessary bring the points closer together by exerting pressure on the *outer* electrode. With "Maglita," magneto models, where the voltage depends to some extent on engine speed, if an excessive gap exists, difficult starting is likely to arise. With coil-ignition models it is not so likely, as the h.t. current is of practically constant voltage. For "Maglita," magneto, and coil models the correct gap is 0·018 in.–0·022 in. (0·025 in.–0·030 in. with suppressor.)

Clean It Frequently. The plug is liable to become oiled up (particularly during the running-in period), sooty or carbonized, and more often than not a combination of all three. Fortunately it is easy to clean, and as a dirty plug immensely affects engine performance you should make a habit of removing the plug fairly frequently and cleaning it. If the plug is not very dirty it is usually sufficient merely to brighten up the electrodes where the spark occurs with the aid of a pen-knife, some fine emery cloth, or a wire-brush cleaner.

About every 2500 miles (or if trouble occurs) a detachable type plug should be dismantled, inspected and thoroughly cleaned.

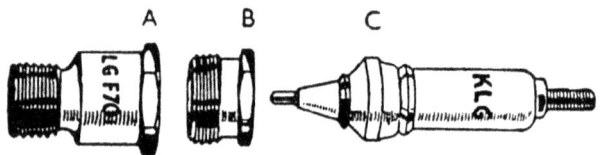

FIG. 25. DETACHABLE TYPE PLUG DISMANTLED FOR THOROUGH CLEANING

Fig. 25 shows a K.L.G. type F70 plug stripped for this purpose. To dismantle the plug hold the hexagon *B* of the gland nut in a vice or spanner. If a vice is used, be careful not to squeeze the hexagon between the jaws. Then, with another spanner, unscrew the large hexagon *A*. The insulated centre electrode *C* can now be detached.

Scrape off all carbon deposits from the metal parts with a small knife, and afterwards rinse the parts in petrol. Do not, however, attempt to scrape the "Sintox" or "Corundite" insulation used on Lodge and K.L.G. plugs respectively.

If the insulation is covered with soft carbon or oil, wash it thoroughly with petrol or paraffin. Afterwards remove all carbon deposits with fairly coarse emery cloth and again wash in petrol or paraffin. Polish the electrode points with some *fine* emery cloth, and reassemble the plug.

When assembling the plug, make sure that there is no grit or dirt lodged between the body of the plug and the insulator of the centre electrode. Also smear a little *thin* oil on the internal washer and make certain that the washer seats correctly, otherwise a gas-tight seal will not be obtained.

The Miller Contact-breaker (Pre-1949). The contact-breaker mounted on the dynamo or on the timing case on pre-1949 coil-ignition models requires periodical attention, but it is inadvisable to interfere with its adjustment unnecessarily. If the ignition

IN THE GARAGE

system is functioning satisfactorily, leave well alone. It is advisable, however, about once every 1000 miles to remove the contact-breaker cover and examine the contacts, and if necessary adjust the gap between them when fully open. This should be between 0·018 in. and 0·020 in. Excessive clearance will affect the ignition timing slightly and may also cause misfiring.

When the contacts are closed (i.e. when the rocker-arm pad leaves the eccentric part of the cam) the contacts should be firmly pressed together by means of the spring. Binding at the rocker-arm pivot bearing will weaken the effect of the spring and prevent the smart make-and-break which is essential to perfect ignition. If the rocker arm works sluggishly, polish and slightly oil both the pivot pin and rocker-arm bearing. Both should be clean and highly polished. It is a good plan also occasionally to smear the cam (A, Fig. 26) with a little petroleum jelly.

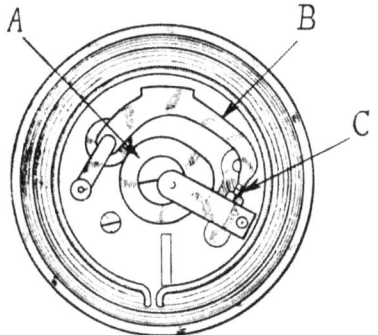

Fig. 26. Contact-breaker on Coil-ignition Models

A = Cam B = Rocker arm
C = Contacts

Examine the contacts closely. When in good condition their surfaces should present a grey, frosted appearance. They must be kept absolutely clean and free from oil, otherwise they are liable to become burnt and perhaps pitted. If bad pitting is present, it may be due to dirty or loose battery connexions or perhaps a faulty condenser. To clean the contacts, rub them with a piece of rag moistened in petrol. To remove slight burning or blackening, clean the contacts with *very fine* emery cloth and afterwards with a rag moistened in petrol. Pitted or uneven contacts will require careful filing with a *dead smooth* file. Only the barest amount of metal must be removed; it facilitates accurate truing up of the contacts if the insulated terminal-post and uninsulated rocker-arm are removed from the contact-breaker and the contacts rubbed on a fine carborundum stone.

If the contact-breaker gap is found excessive, rotate the engine slowly until the contacts are fully open, and then with the small contact-breaker spanner in the tool kit loosen the locknut securing the adjustable-contact screw, and turn the screw until the feeler gauge on the spanner just goes between the contacts without binding. Keep the coil terminal-cap clean. (See also page 84.)

How to Test Miller Condenser. If the contacts of the Miller contact-breaker quickly become pitted or burnt you should test

50 THE BOOK OF THE PANTHER (LIGHTWEIGHT)

for a faulty condenser (fortunately a rare occurrence). The condenser, which is housed on the back of the contact-breaker cover, should be removed and a lighting main's voltage applied to its terminals. To avoid a short-circuit in the event of the condenser proving defective or breaking down under the test, a lamp should be

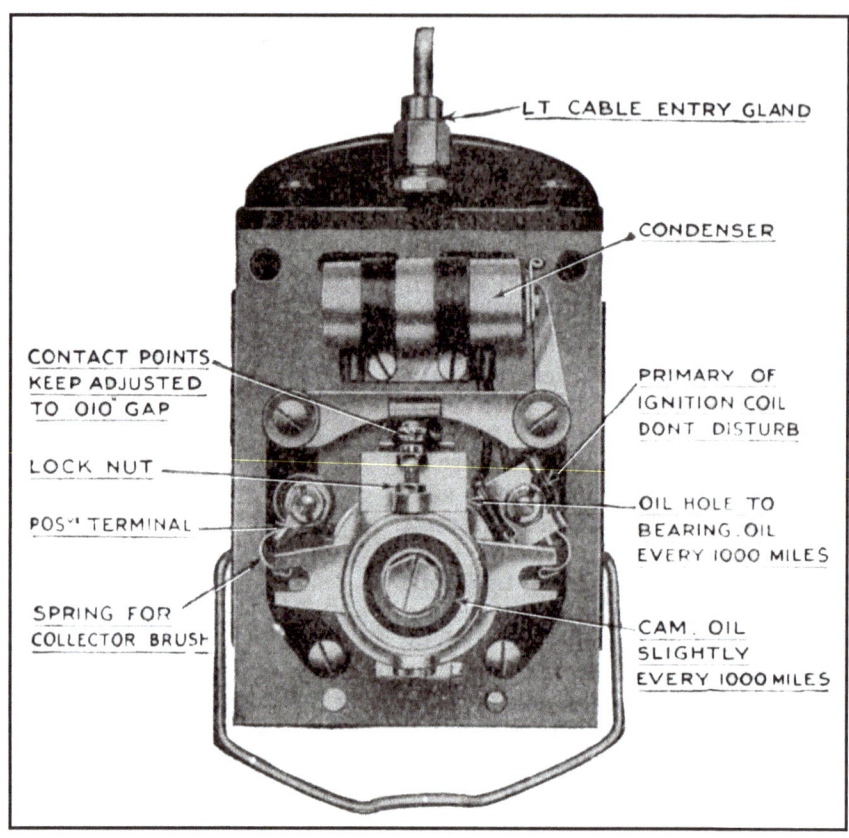

FIG. 27. CONTACT-BREAKER ON LUCAS "MAGLITA"
With this instrument the lighting and ignition are quite independent

connected in series. If the condenser is not at fault, on removing the voltage a fairly "fat" spark will be obtained when the condenser terminals are short-circuited, even after the lapse of a few seconds. If the condenser is at fault it will be impossible to get a spark. Note: novices should *never* experiment with lighting mains.

The "Maglita" Contact-breaker (Pre-1949). On Red Panther "Maglita" equipment examine the contact-breaker (Fig. 27) occasionally and if the contacts are oily or dirty clean them with a rag damped in petrol. The gap between the contacts should be adjusted if necessary until there is a clearance of 0·010 in., which is the thickness of the gauge on the contact-breaker spanner provided in the tool kit. After loosening the locknut (see Fig. 27) the adjustable-contact screw can be turned as required. Pitted contacts should be trued up with a *dead smooth* file or emery cloth. Finally do not forget the lubrication hints given in the illustration.

Burman Clutch Adjustment (1934-48). All 1934-48 models have Burman gearboxes and clutches; the clutch assembly is shown sectioned in Fig. 28. Should clutch slip be experienced (usually indicated by intermittent engine racing and heating up of the clutch plates), an adjustment should at once be made. At all times there must be a little backlash at the handlebar lever. If the clutch begins to slip, first suspect the clutch cable adjustment and if necessary adjust until there is the requisite $\frac{1}{32}$ in. clearance between the clutch rod and the ball in the actuating lever. If the cable adjuster is already screwed right home, the necessary clearance can usually be obtained by unscrewing the adjuster screw H (Fig. 28) a trifle. Should clutch slip persist, it is possible that the cork inserts have become badly worn or damaged, or that the spring adjusters K require tightening up, and each of these should be given half a turn, when a test should be made. If necessary, repeat but be careful to tighten all the adjusters evenly. They should not be screwed up hard but should be just flush with the spring plate (about seven turns from right home).

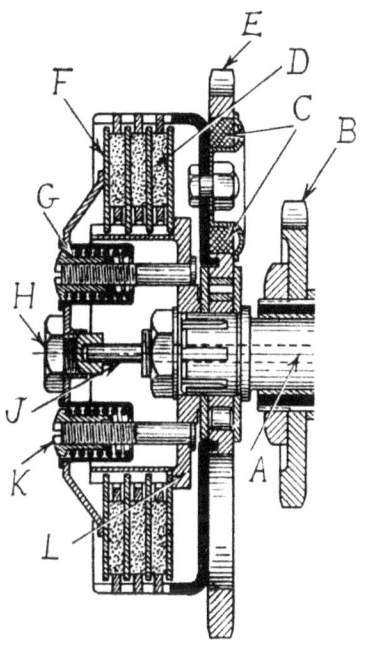

Fig. 28. Sectional View of 1934-48 Burman Clutch

A = Gearbox mainshaft
B = Gearbox sprocket
C = Rubber buffers
D = Cork insert plates
E = Clutch sprocket
F = Driven plates
G = Clutch springs
H = Adjuster screw and locknut
J = Clutch rod
K = Spring adjuster nut
L = Clutch body

Should the clutch be difficult to free in spite of the cable not having stretched, wear may have occurred on the clutch rod J in which case the adjuster screw H should be slightly tightened (if it is not fully tightened already). A tendency for the clutch spring adjusters to become unscrewed usually means that the springs have become rusted or dirty and the remedy is to clean the springs and grease them. If relative movement develops between the clutch sprocket and case, it indicates that the rubber buffers C are worn and require replacement. A tendency for both the clutch sprocket and case to "rock" from side to side indicates that the roller race inside the clutch sprocket needs new rollers. Only about $\frac{1}{64}$ in. end play is permissible. Excessive play may cause the tongues on the clutch plates to wear grooves in the clutch case. Dirty or oily plates should be cleaned with petrol. For 1949-58 clutch, see page 89.

Sturmey-Archer Clutch (Pre-1934). Sturmey-Archer gearboxes and clutches are fitted on 1932-3 models and in order to avoid clutch slip it is important to maintain about $\frac{1}{16}$ in. free movement between the actuating lever above the kick-starter and the clutch rod. If this movement, which is essential to proper engagement of the plates, is not present, the Bowden cable stop should be adjusted accordingly. It may, however, be necessary in order to obtain the desired adjustment to loosen the lever actuating screw a trifle. The three-speed models have single spring clutches and the four-speed models multi-spring clutches. Keep the spring screws fully tightened on the latter. Adjustment of the clutch will most likely be needed during the first 1000 miles as new cables are apt to stretch considerably.

Gear Control (Pre-1945). An adjustment of the primary chain tension by pivoting the gearbox backwards or forwards invariably upsets the adjustment of the gear control (except where foot control is provided), and this must at once be attended to. Incorrect adjustment causes rattle of the gear lever in its quadrant in second gear notch, and perhaps a tendency for the lever to jump right out and cause serious damage. On Sturmey-Archer gearbox models remove the pin from the top connexion of the long rod and rotate the yoke until on reconnecting it the gear lever is placed centrally in the top-gear quadrant notch with top gear engaged. Burman gearboxes have internal indexing and it is possible to feel when a gear engages. On Burman gearbox models adjust the length so that the lever is centrally placed in the *second gear* quadrant notch with second gear engaged.

No Adjustment for Transmission Shock-absorber. An engine shaft shock-absorber is used on 1932-3 three-speed Red Panthers and 1945-58 P. & M. Panthers to damp out any tendency for transmission snatch, but on 1934-39 models, except 1939-40 Model 40, the transmission shock-absorber is incorporated in the Burman clutch. In neither case is any adjustment required, although in the case of the clutch shock-absorber renewal

IN THE GARAGE 53

of the rubber discs may be necessary after covering a very big mileage.

Correct Chain Tension is Very Important. A watchful eye should always be kept on the tension of both primary and secondary chains, and an adjustment made if necessary. If the chains are slack they tend to rattle and may jump the sprocket teeth and perhaps cause serious damage. It is in fact quite possible for carelessness in regard to chain tension to land a rider in a hospital or mortuary! New chains stretch very considerably and excessive whip must be remedied as soon as it is noticed. Also avoid running with the chains excessively taut, as this is likely to damage

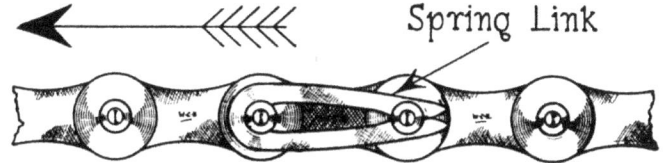

FIG. 29. HOW TO FIT A CHAIN SPRING LINK

To minimize the risk of a chain parting the spring link should always be fitted as shown. To facilitate connecting a chain, join the ends on the rear-wheel sprocket

the chain rollers and also the teeth of the gearbox and clutch sprockets.

To Retension Primary Chain (1932-48). Automatically lubricated on all models and on some models totally enclosed in an oil-bath chain case, it stretches somewhat slower than in the case of the secondary chain which is more exposed, but nevertheless it will need occasional retensioning—probably not during the first 1000 miles. To do this, first slacken off the large clinch nut on the off-side of the gearbox and on the outside of the engine plate. Also slacken the nut on the lower fixing-bolt on which the gearbox is pivoted. In the case of 1932-4 models pull the gearbox backwards by turning the hexagon sleeve on the push-and-pull type chain adjuster (connected to the top gearbox bolt) *anticlockwise* until the correct chain tension is obtained. On 1935 and later models a double cam adjustment is provided, and the beauty of this is that it ensures permanent chain alinement. In this case turn the upper bolt by means of the squared end until the chain is correctly tensioned. If it is necessary to slacken the chain, be careful when moving the gearbox to see that the cams bear against the pegs in the engine plates.

The primary chain should be tensioned, and kept tensioned, so that it is possible to deflect it at the centre with the fingers to the extent of ⅜ in. to ½ in. On oil-bath chain case models it is not necessary to detach the outer half of the case as the fingers can be slipped through the hole exposed on removing the inspection disc. After retensioning the chain, again tighten the gearbox fixing-bolt nuts securely and check over the gear control, and if necessary adjust. For 1949-58 models, see page 89.

To Retension Secondary Chain. The rear chain requires retensioning at regular intervals, according to the mileage of the machine and the care with which the chain has been lubricated (see page 36). When correctly tensioned, it should be possible to

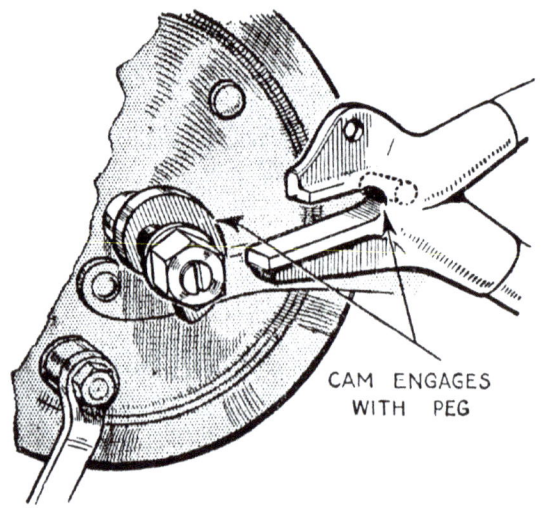

FIG. 30. CAM ADJUSTMENT FOR THE SECONDARY CHAIN
(See note on page 90)

deflect the chain ½ in. to ¾ in. at its centre. To retension the chain slacken the finger adjustment of the rear-brake rod and also the two spindle nuts. Then turn the spindle by means of its squared end until the eccentric cam (Fig. 30) draws the rear wheel backwards the necessary amount. It is important to make sure that both cams bear against the pegs provided in the fork ends. Also avoid letting the wheel spindle come dangerously near the end of the fork ends; if the chain has stretched very badly remove a link.

Do Not Bother About Wheel Alinement. You need not bother yourself about front and rear wheel alinement as the cam adjustment for the rear wheel spindle (Fig. 30) automatically ensures

IN THE GARAGE

that alinement is not upset—provided, of course, that you have not been too intimate with a vehicle and twisted the frame!

Wheel Bearings. All Red Panthers, except 1939-40 Model 40, have cup and cone type hub bearings for both wheels and, if the spindle nuts are kept done up tightly and the hubs are adequately lubricated (see page 38), there is little likelihood of adjustment being called for until you have covered many thousands of miles. The bearings should not be over-tightened or damaged balls and ball races may result. Side play (at the rim) amounting to about $\frac{1}{32}$ in. is permissible and even advisable, but there should be no play in excess of this. If excessive play develops, slacken the locknut and locking washer, and screw inwards slightly the adjusting cone (R.H. thread) which is situated on the near-side of the machine. It will be found necessary to remove the locking washer before the adjusting nut can be turned. Test for free running by spinning each wheel. No adjustment is provided for 1945-58 Panthers.

To Remove Front Wheel. Disconnect the brake cable "U" piece from the brake anchor-plate lever, slacken both spindle nuts and lift the wheel out, springing the fork blades apart slightly while doing so. Instructions for 1949 and later Panthers with Dowty "Oleomatic" or Panther front forks are given on pages 91–92.

To Remove Rear Wheel. On numerous models the rear portion of the mudguard is hinged. Slacken the two nuts on the two bolts passing through the mudguard valance and lift the tail-piece up. Then disconnect the rear-brake rod and the secondary chain, loosen the spindle nuts, and gently ease the rear wheel out of the fork ends.

Hints on Tyre Repairs. Probably you have had some kind of experience in this matter and the author will only mention a few hints. Punctures are a rare occurrence nowadays, and if tyre pressures are kept correct (page 9) it is very unlikely that you will often have occasion to open the repair outfit. Punctures can frequently be saved by occasional scrutiny of the treads and digging out with a small knife any flints or stones embedded in the rubber. When removing a cover, always begin *well away from the valve* and use the tyre levers firmly but gently. Use autovulcanizing type patches such as the Dunlop "Vulcafix." Apply the solution to the tube only. Test the tube afterwards if possible by partially inflating it and immersing it in a basin of water. Before refitting, dab it liberally with french chalk, and when replacing the cover see that the valve is pushed squarely home.

Slight inflation will often assist refitting of the cover, the wire edges of which must be pushed right down into the sides of the well-base rim. See also notes on page 101.

Brake Adjustment. Brake linings gradually wear and an adjustment becomes necessary. Simple adjustment is provided for both brakes and there is thus no excuse for not keeping them adjusted to give maximum braking efficiency. If the brakes happen to get oily the shoes should be removed and the linings cleaned with petrol. Harsh brakes can often be cured by filing down each lining for about 1 in. from each end. Fitting new linings is simple as they are obtainable with the rivet holes already drilled in them. The rivet heads must be quite flush. See page 92.

Adjusting Steering Head. During the running-in period the ball races in the frame and on the fork crown settle somewhat, and any play that may have arisen in these bearings can be detected by applying the front brake with the handlebar lever, and with both wheels on the ground rocking the machine to and fro. The play can be actually *felt* if a finger is placed over the ball head lug. There might also be a little backlash at the front-brake anchor plate lever, and this must be taken into account when adjusting the steering-head bearing.

To Take Up Play in the Steering Head (1932-46). First slacken off the cotter nut on the left-hand side of the ball head, punch back the cotter slightly, and screw down the large nut which forms the base of the steering head. Do not, however, turn this nut more than a quarter of a turn at a time, because if the bearing is excessively tightened it will set up a rolling action in the steering. To adjust steering, 1947 onwards, see page 93.

The Steering Damper. Adjust the steering damper (fitted on some Red Panthers) while riding to suit conditions, and keep it slackened right off except when indulging in fast riding.

Handlebar Adjustment. These are designed to be adjustable to suit your physical make-up, and it is worth while finding out if they are actually adjusted to give the greatest comfort. If not, slacken the clamping bolts and adjust as desired (see page 82).

Fork Spindles (Pre-1947). On new machines the enamel on the clearance washers between the side links and fork girder becomes rubbed off and some side play gradually develops. This end play caused through any other reason can be remedied by slackening the locknuts on both ends of the spindle, and giving the spindle a

IN THE GARAGE

quarter of a turn in an *anti-clockwise* direction after which the locknut on the near-side of the machine should be firmly tightened up, and then the locknut at the opposite end should also be tightened. Before carrying out these adjustments slacken the shock absorbers as much as possible, and then test the movement of the forks so as to make certain that the spindle and link are not binding. Adjust each spindle in turn and see that the small knurled washers are free to revolve without end float. (See pages 77-81.)

Keep Carburettor Controls Sensitive. It makes a lot of difference to running if there is no backlash in the carburettor controls and the slides should begin to respond immediately the air lever and twist-grip are operated. Whenever necessary take up cable stretch by means of the two adjusters on the mixing chamber cap.

DECARBONIZING AND VALVE GRINDING

Decarbonize only when the engine needs it, normally at intervals of approximately 4000-5000 miles. After 4000-5000 miles an engine usually exhibits signs indicating that it is advisable to decarbonize it. Gone is that youthful vivacity and power, and probably the machine begins to shy at quite ordinary gradients up which it normally romps in a care-free manner and shows its disapproval in no uncertain way by emitting a knocking or pinking noise. Accompanying these objectionable symptoms is a change from a crisp exhaust note to one which is distinctly "woolly" and tells you that the engine is not in a healthy condition. As soon as the engine behaves (or rather misbehaves) in the above manner, and especially if unprovoked knocking is apt to occur, you should dry-dock the machine, remove the cylinder and/or the cylinder head and decarbonize the engine and grind-in the valves if necessary. The last mentioned usually require attention every alternate decarbonizing. Decarbonizing is a long word, but the actual job is quite a short one and presents no difficulties. Avoid removing the cylinder *barrel* each time the engine is decarbonized.

What are Carbon Deposits Due To? Carbon deposits are due to a combination of three things: (*a*) burnt lubricating oil; (*b*) carbonizing of road dust; (*c*) incomplete fuel combustion. When decarbonizing it is always worth while inspecting the valve seatings and, *if necessary*, grinding-in the valves. Removal of the valves incidentally facilitates thorough cleaning of the ports.

Getting Ready for the Job. Put the machine on its stand and get out the tool kit. Also have at hand a valve-spring compressor, a valve grinding tool, a tin of valve grinding paste, a blunt screwdriver, new gudgeon-pin circlips, a jar containing paraffin, some clean rags, some clean paper on which to lay the parts, some engine oil, and you are about "all set." Is the engine dirty outside as well as inside? If it is, it is very advisable to give it a clean with a rag and paraffin, being particularly careful to clean thoroughly those parts about to be dismantled. Put the piston at the top of the firing stroke so that both valves are completely closed, and then get down to the business of stripping the engine.

Petrol Tank Removal is Necessary. Although decarbonizing can be done without removing the petrol tank, in the case of 1932-4 models with separate cylinder head and rocker-box, there is no question but that the job is enormously facilitated by preliminary removal of the tank—and this is very simple. Disconnect the petrol pipe(s) and gear lever (if fitted) by removing the yoke pin and then remove the front and rear tank-fixing bolts, when the tank can be gently lifted off. Be careful not to lose the rubber insulation buffers, metal washers, and split-pins.

" Clearing the Deck." The next step is to remove those parts which hinder dismantling proper. Remove the exhaust pipe and silencer (duplicated in the case of twin-port models) by unscrewing the finned pipe nut (fitted on all recent models) at the port with a ring spanner (extra) and removing the bolts which secure the silencer to the frame lugs. Disconnect the carburettor petrol pipe(s) from both carburettor and tank (below the tap) and proceed to remove the carburettor. To do this, unscrew the knurled ring on the mixing chamber and pull out both the throttle and air slides; then remove the two set-bolts holding the carburettor to the inlet port and put the carburettor body complete with float chamber safely on one side for cleaning (page 21). Disconnect the lead from the plug and remove the latter. See also page 93.

To Remove Rocker-box (1932-4 Models). 1932-4 Red Panthers have separate rocker-boxes and cylinder heads, unlike later models which have the two combined. To remove the rocker-box from the cylinder head, first of all remove the rocker-box end plate complete with exhaust-valve lifter (see Fig. 22) by undoing the six screws and allow it to hang on the end of the Bowden cable, preferably tucked away near the handlebars. Then remove the four rocker-box fixing screws and the two screws at the base of the push-rod cover. On 1934 models disconnect the oil pipe. It is now possible to remove the rocker-box together with the push-rods and cover tube from the vertical flange on the cylinder head. Do not break the joint between the cover tube and rocker-box, and if this is done by accident, jointing compound must be used on reassembly.

To Remove Cylinder Head (1932-4 Models). After detaching the rocker-box, the cylinder head bolts from beneath the cylinder fins should be removed with the box spanner provided in the tool kit, and the cylinder head lifted off the cylinder spigot. The joint is of the metal-to-metal type with no gasket interposed, and should the cylinder head be difficult to remove due to burnt carbon deposits, apply a piece of hard wood to the underside of the inlet and exhaust ports and tap gently upwards with a *light* hammer.

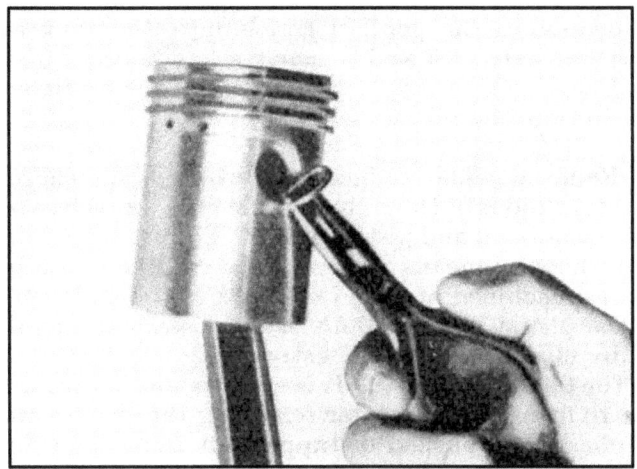

FIG. 31. REMOVING GUDGEON-PIN CIRCLIP WITH THE SMALL PLIERS (PROVIDED IN RED PANTHER TOOL KIT)

It is advisable to remove both circlips and it is necessary to fit new ones when refitting the piston

On no account try to drive a wedge or chisel between the cylinder and cylinder head faces. Lay the cylinder head carefully on one side as it is made of cast-iron and easily fractured. Also block up the cylinder bore with a piece of clean rag to prevent the highly polished interior from being scratched.

To Remove Cylinder Head and Rocker-box (1935 to 1948). First remove on 1935-7 models the rocker-box end plate. On later models disconnect the exhaust-valve lifter (page 73) and remove rocker-box cover; also disconnect at both ends the oil pipe(s) to the rocker-box by unscrewing the union nuts at the crankcase and rocker-box. Then unscrew the screws holding the telescopic push-rod cover flange and remove rocker-box and cylinder head together (see above). Also remove push-rods (see page 94).

Drawing Off Cylinder Barrel. When the cylinder head is removed, it is a simple matter to draw off (see notes on page 94) the cylinder barrel after removing the four fixing nuts. When withdrawing the barrel the engine should be turned over until the piston is at the bottom of its stroke, and the barrel gently eased off, care being taken to prevent the loose piston falling sharply against the connecting-rod which might damage or distort the skirt of the aluminium-alloy piston. If you damage the cylinder base washer a new one will be required.

When removing the cylinder do not neglect to wrap a rag around the base of the piston, so as not to allow any dirt or foreign matter to enter the crankcase. Remember, that should you by accident drop even the smallest article into the crankcase it will be necessary to extract it and this may entail hours of unnecessary trouble. Before commencing to remove the piston-rings it is the best plan to take the piston right off.

Piston Removal. The gudgeon-pin which holds the piston on the connecting-rod is of the fully-floating type, i.e. is free to revolve in both the small-end and piston bosses. The pin is held in position on the Panthers by means of two special circlips which bed down into grooves machined at each outer end of the gudgeon-pin hole through the piston bosses. Both of these steel circlips should be removed by closing the ends together with a pair of snipe-nosed pliers (in the tool kit, 1932-9). It is essential not to use the circlips again but to fit new ones. After removing the circlips the hollow gudgeon-pin can be pushed or tapped out from one side and the piston taken off (see also page 94). The piston laps out the cylinder in which it reciprocates in a certain manner depending upon the piston thrust, lubrication and other factors, and it is never advisable to refit it except in its original position on the connecting-rod. In other words, it should not be reversed back to front and vice versa. On the inside of the rear (thrust) face of some pistons a small V groove is cut, and this identification, or any others, can therefore be used as a guide to ensure correct reassembly. If the piston is unmarked, scratch an "F" inside to indicate the front. Be very careful with the piston, as it is easily distorted.

Piston Rings are Very Fragile. Great care must be taken when removing the piston rings as they are made of cast-iron and are exceedingly brittle. It is unsafe to spring them out wider than the diameter of the piston crown, and the safest method of removing the three rings is shown in Fig. 32. Three strips of sheet tin about 2 in. long and $\frac{3}{8}$ in. wide are inserted under the rings at even distances, enabling the rings to be gently eased off one by one. A proprietary tool will answer the same purpose. Be careful with the oil control ring and do not damage the piston-ring lands.

The Piston Rings. The rings should be polished round the whole of their surfaces, and if either ring is discoloured or has a black patch on it it means that gas has been leaking past, and it should therefore be replaced by a new one. With the rings removed the piston should be washed, so that the degree of carbon deposit in the grooves may be readily seen. If any is found here it should be scraped away, but extreme care is necessary in order that the surface of the groove is not damaged by the scraping tool. If it is,

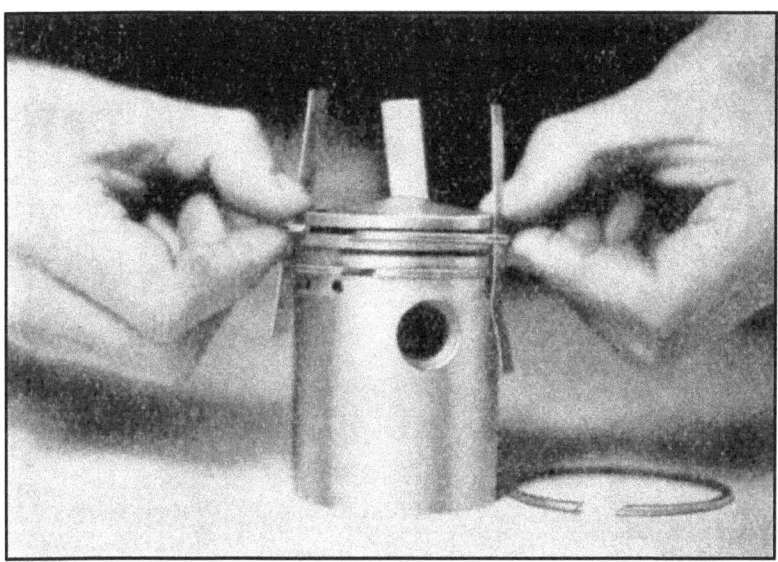

FIG. 32. A REALLY SAFE METHOD OF REMOVING PISTON RINGS
This method (see text) can also be used for refitting rings

loss of compression will result, and if the groove is badly cut or dented a new piston will probably have to be fitted to restore maximum efficiency. Any carbon deposits on the inside of the rings should be scraped off. It is important to see that the rings are quite free in their grooves but have no appreciable up and down movement. The piston and rings must again be washed in paraffin, after the carbon deposits have been removed.

Refitting the rings is quite simple. Before this is done a few drops of oil should be placed in the grooves and the top ring may then be pushed over the top of the piston until it is home, followed by the other two rings. Alternatively, the method shown in Fig. 32

may be used. See that the piston ring gaps are spaced at equal distances. On the Panther three-ring piston they should be spaced at 120 degrees. The correct piston-ring gaps (with the rings in the cylinder) are 0·006 in., for top and middle plain rings, and 0·006 in. in respect of the bottom oil-control ring. The respective gaps for 1949-58 are 0·010 in. and 0·011 in.

Removing Carbon Deposits. Thoroughness in decarbonizing well repays the labour expended. The more completely the carbon is removed, the better will engine performance be, and the longer will it be before decarbonizing again becomes necessary. It is

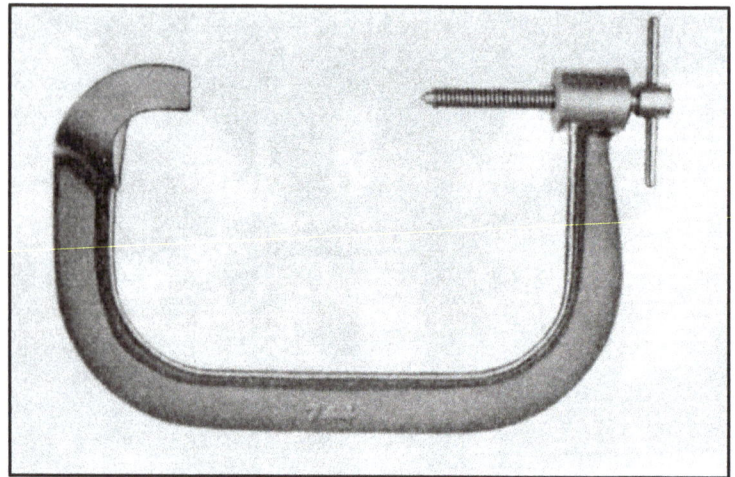

Fig. 33. The Panther Valve-spring Compressor

inadvisable, however, to decarbonize the piston-ring grooves more than about once every alternate decarbonizing, when the valves should also be ground-in. When undertaking an ordinary top overhaul, only the carbon deposits on the piston crown, inside the exhaust port, and the head combustion-chamber need be scraped off. To do this, a suitable scraper such as a blunt edged screwdriver should be employed. Be careful, however, not to employ excessive force on the piston, otherwise the comparatively soft aluminium alloy may be deeply scratched. After chipping off all carbon deposits from the top of the piston, clean it with paraffin and then polish the crown of the piston with a soft cloth. Leave the sides of the piston well alone (including the lands between the grooves).

When decarbonizing the cylinder head, scrape the combustion chamber *before* removing the valves, and clean the exhaust port

IN THE GARAGE

after removing the valves. See that the face of the cylinder head is not scratched. If you wish, you may polish the combustion chamber with fine emery cloth, but this must not *on any account* be done to the piston. Afterwards clean with paraffin.

To Remove the Valves. With the cylinder head removed (complete with rocker-box on 1935 to 1948 models) the valves can be worked at in comfort on a bench, table, or other suitable spot. For a very modest sum most accessory dealers supply a really excellent valve-spring compressor. The method of using this tool,

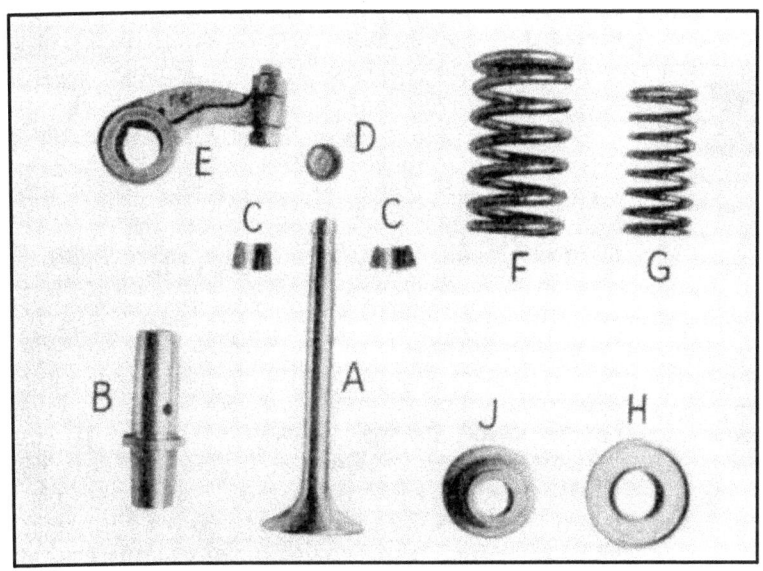

Fig. 34. Group of Valve Parts Dismantled

A = Valve
B = Valve guide
C = Split collet
D = Valve stem end-cap (1932-4)
E = O.H. rocker (1932-4)
F = Outer valve-spring
G = Inner valve-spring
H = Valve-spring lower collar
J = Valve-spring upper collar

after removing the hardened valve stem end-caps (1932-4 models) and pushing the O.H. rockers out of the way, is to place the forked end of the tool over the valve-spring collar and the pointed end of the screw in the centre of the valve head and screw up until the valve-spring is compressed sufficiently to enable the split collet to be removed. If stuck, gently tap it out. The valve-spring collars, duplex valve-spring and valve can then be removed. Deal with each valve in this manner. After removing the valves be careful not to interchange them because, although both valves are made of the same steel and are of the same pattern, each valve is individually ground on to its seat and will not as a rule provide a perfect gas-tight seal unless kept in the seat on which it was originally ground-in. It is usually possible to identify the exhaust valve readily as this almost invariably is discoloured more than the inlet valve. After removing the valves and placing the parts on a clean sheet of paper, clean the valve stems and rub down any high spots with *very fine* emery cloth, doing this with a lengthwise movement.

How to Grind-in the Valves. Should the valve faces or seats show signs of serious pitting, the valves should be ground-in. The overhead valves on the Panther engines have, of course, to be rotated and lightly pressed down against their seatings by means of a suction-type valve grinding tool such as that shown in Fig. 35.

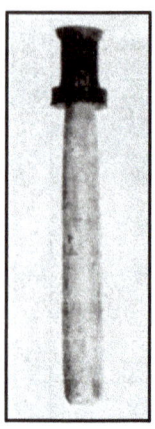

Fig. 35. Grinding Tool

Grind-in valves only when necessary, using a ready-made compound such as Richford's grinding paste. Do not apply the paste like jam on bread and butter, but with a rag apply just a *thin* film around the bevelled edge of the valve head. Also do not after inserting the valve in its guide rotate the valve round and round with the valve grinding tool, but rotate it about a third of a turn in one direction and then an equal amount in the opposite direction. About every half-dozen oscillations lift the valve off its seat, rotate it about a third of a revolution and continue grinding-in; this should be proceeded with until no "cut" can be felt, when further grinding paste should be applied and the valve face and seating cleaned and examined.

Continue grinding-in until both the valve face and the head seating have a matt finish. Perfect ring contact is not good enough and there should be some depth of perfect seating. Extreme care must be taken after grinding-in to remove *all* traces of grinding paste. As previously mentioned, the valve stems may be cleaned up with very fine or, better still, worn emery cloth. Do not be in too much of a hurry. The use of fine grade grinding paste is preferable and gives much better results than using a coarse grade, although if pitting is deep and extensive the use of the latter may be necessitated first. Care should be taken not to damage the valve stems in any way, otherwise the valves may not move freely in their guides.

The reason why valves should not be ground-in unnecessarily is because this tends to make them sink or become "pocketed" in their seats, with the result that resistance is offered to the smooth passage of the ingoing and outgoing gases. It is quite

IN THE GARAGE

sufficient to remove all pitting from the valves and seats, but should the valves and their seats happen to be very deeply pitted (which a reasonable amount of valve grinding will not remove) the proper procedure is to return the cylinder head and valves to a repairer (page 83) to have the valve faces and seats recut. Before reassembling the valves test them for fit in the valve guides. If the inlet valve is a sloppy fit (0·004 in. is minimum clearance) a new valve guide should be fitted, but this is only necessary after a big mileage. A worn inlet-valve guide upsets carburation and causes difficult starting, blow-back through the carburettor and loss of power. Sometimes it is enough to fit a new valve.

Renewing Valve Springs. It is not necessary to fit new valve springs every time the engine is decarbonized or the valves ground-in. Owing to their robust design, the valve springs are quite capable of service in the neighbourhood of 10,000 miles. It should be understood, however, that if a spring shows signs of undue closing and consequent weakening, it should be replaced immediately. "Aero" valve springs (obtainable from most of the motor-cycle accessory firms) are specially recommended for Panther engines (see also notes on page 97).

Reassembling Valves. After grinding-in the valves you should reassemble them in the correct guides, but before doing this poke a piece of thin wire down the oil channels in the cylinder head to ensure their being unobstructed. Smear the valve stems with oil and replace them in their guides. Then refit the duplex valve springs and collars, being careful not to mix up the upper and lower collars (see Fig. 34). Next compress each valve spring with the valve-spring compressor and refit the split collet, making certain that it beds down properly. The application of a little grease to the lower part of the valve stem facilitates reassembly, as this enables the split collet to stick on the valve stem while compressing the springs. Finally do not forget to replace the (1932-4) valve stem end-caps, and if these are seriously worn, renew, otherwise side thrust will be imposed by the rockers on the valves and the guides will wear.

After the Valves Are Reassembled. It is an excellent plan to test the seats by pouring some petrol into the ports and watching for leakage past the valves. Not the slightest sign of moisture should creep past the valves until after a considerable time has elapsed. If some petrol quickly gets past the valves it is sure proof that the valves have not been sufficiently ground-in and the remedy is (horrible thought!) remove and continue grinding-in.

Cleaning Cylinder Finning. Rain and heat quickly cause the cylinder fins of an air-cooled engine to become rusty. This does not appreciably affect the running, but it becomes an eyesore, and to a small extent reduces heat radiation. To remedy this, clean the cylinder fins with a stiff brush soaked in paraffin, and afterwards paint the fins (cast-iron) with cylinder black which can be obtained at any accessory dealer.

Refitting Piston and Cylinder Barrel. This should be done in the reverse order of dismantling. Smear both the piston and inside of the cylinder barrel with engine oil and refit the piston the correct way round (page 60) on the connecting-rod, pushing the gudgeon-pin (see page 94), also oiled, home, after fitting a *new* circlip to one piston boss. Fit a new circlip (see Fig. 31) opposite to it (you cannot be sure the old one is perfect) and see that it beds down properly in the piston-boss groove and is fully expanded. Remember that if a circlip "goes west" with the engine running you may have to put your hand in your pocket for a new piston and cylinder barrel. Then examine the cylinder base washer. If this is in any way damaged, replace it and be absolutely sure that the oil hole (see Fig. 36) in the pre-1949 paper washer coincides with the oil holes in the cylinder flange and mouth of the crankcase. Also see that the cylinder barrel spigot, washer, and mouth of the crankcase are scrupulously clean, and do not omit to clean out the oil hole from the cylinder flange to the inside of the cylinder with a piece of wire before replacing the cylinder barrel.

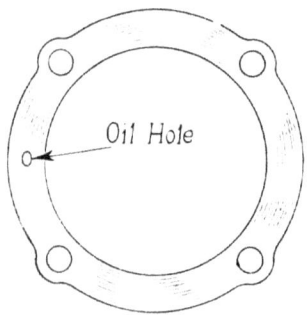

FIG. 36. SEE THAT THIS WASHER IS CORRECTLY REPLACED (PRE-1949)
Unless the oil hole faces the rear as shown, the engine will be starved of oil

To replace the barrel* put the piston well down, space the rings properly (see page 62), hold the cylinder barrel over the piston with one hand and offer the piston up to it with the other, squeezing the rings (without upsetting the position of the gaps) together until the complete piston enters the cylinder barrel. Avoid putting any side strain on either the piston or connecting-rod. After seeing that the spigot beds down on the crankcase squarely and closely, tighten up the four cylinder-barrel nuts finger-tight first and then securely with a spanner in a diagonal order. Even tightening is important, otherwise there is some risk

* Before this is done, you should, if the sump has been drained (page 30), **pour some oil over the flywheels.**

IN THE GARAGE

of distorting the cylinder flange and preventing its bedding down properly on the crankcase. No jointing compound should be used at the base of the cylinder, but a pre-1949 washer if replaced by a new one should be oiled first.

A Check on Oil Circulation. It is a good plan with the cylinder barrel in position to verify that the oil pump is functioning satisfactorily. On 1932-5 models turn the oil regulator full on. By kicking the engine over several times it is possible to see whether oil issues from the hole in the rear of the cylinder wall. It is presumed, of course, that the oil filter is in position and the oil sump is amply replenished. (See also page 28.)

Refitting Cylinder Head (1932-4 Models). Before this is done the cylinder barrel and head faces must be scraped absolutely clean. A little jointing compound such as Hermetite or Gasket Goo should then be smeared on both the faces to ensure a gas-tight joint being made. The head can then be lowered on to the barrel spigot, care being taken to verify that it beds down properly. Screw up the four fixing nuts below the fins evenly with the box key provided and you are ready for refitting the rocker-box. To replace the 1949-58 cylinder head, see page 97.

Refitting Rocker-box, Push-rods, etc. (1932-4 Models). It is presumed that the rocker-box has been reassembled or has not been dismantled other than removal of the end plate complete with exhaust-valve lifter. Clean the rocker-box flange and the vertical flange on the cylinder head and smear some jointing compound on them, being *most* careful not to allow any of it to get into the oil holes leading to the valve guides (see Fig. 22). If the upper push-rod cover joint has been disturbed, some jointing compound should be used here also (see page 59).

Replace the rocker-box complete with push-rods and push-rod cover. This is easily done if the push-rods are first lowered into the timing case so that the ball ends fit snugly into the recesses in the cam levers, and by lowering the assembly until the flange of the push-rod cover tube rests on the crankcase the push-rod upper cups can easily be guided with the thumb and forefinger until they fit over the rocker-arm balls (slight rotation of the rocker-box will facilitate this). When refitting the push-rods make sure that the piston is in a position such that both valves are fully closed, and the cam levers therefore lying parallel with each other. Replace the two rocker-box fixing bolts and the cover-tube flange screws, tightening each up a little at a time. Also on 1934 models reconnect the oil feed-pipe. The rocker-box cover complete with exhaust valve lifter can now be refitted and screwed up tightly in position. Afterwards do not forget to check the exhaust-valve lifter adjustment. The carburettor, plug, petrol pipe, exhaust pipe(s), silencer(s), and finally the petrol tank can now be replaced. Check the valve clearances (page 44) and the engine is ready for the road. It should now be very lively, no longer "woolly." After a little running, again go over the engine nuts and bolts with a spanner.

Refitting Cylinder Head, Rocker-box, etc. (1935 to 1948). On 1935 and later models the cylinder head and rocker-box are integral and are removed together. See that the barrel and head faces are quite clean and smear with jointing compound or replace gasket (1939 onwards). Verify that the piston is in a position such that both tappets are fully closed, slip the push-rods inside the cover tube and hold the push-rod cupped ends on the rocker-arm balls. The telescopic push-rod cover tube together (separately if preferred) with the cylinder head and integral rocker-box should then be placed in position. See that the lower ball ends of the push-rods engage with the cupped tappet-heads, check the tappet adjustment (page 44) and screw the telescopic push-rod cover flange on to the crankcase. Tighten down all the cylinder head nuts evenly and diagonally, refit the rocker-box cover, reconnect the rocker-box oil pipe(s), valve lifter and reassemble such items as the carburettor, plug, petrol pipe, exhaust pipe(s), silencer(s) and lastly the petrol tank. Reassembly is now complete. Start the engine up after again checking and, if necessary, adjusting the valve clearances (see page 44) and draining and replenishing the sump (page 30). After 20 miles running go over the various engine nuts and bolts and give a half-turn or so with a spanner if slack. Check valve clearances. (For 1949-58 see page 97.)

HINTS ON GENERAL OVERHAUL

After a big mileage, preferably in the dull winter months and not during the summer when the sun and fresh air urge you to get on the road, you should give your Panther a very careful and complete overhaul. Strip the machine right down, clean all the parts, examine them minutely and make such replacements and adjustments as are necessary. It is best to take the engine and gearbox right out of the frame. In this book the complete overhaul can only briefly be touched on, but the following hints may prove useful. (See also page 98.)

Where to Look for Trouble. Special points to be noted in the complete overhaul are set out herewith—
  FRAME. Alinement, existence of flaws or cracks, play in

IN THE GARAGE

fork-bearings, looseness of steering head, wear caused by friction of all attached parts, condition of rear-suspension units, and enamel.

WHEELS. Condition of cup and cone or journal bearings, truth

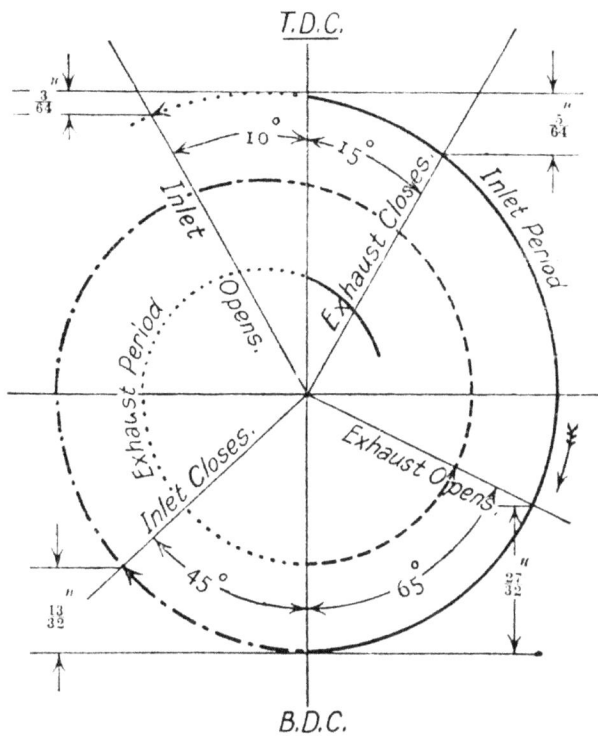

FIG. 37. VALVE TIMING DIAGRAM FOR 1932-58 248 C.C. AND 1932-53 348 C.C. PANTHER ENGINES

On 1938 and later engines 10° (I.O.), 45° (I.C.), 65° (E.O.), and 15° (E.C.) are equivalent to $\frac{3}{64}$ in., $\frac{1}{2}$ in., 1 in. and $\frac{5}{64}$ in. where the measurement is taken on the piston stroke

of wheels, alinement, loose spokes, condition of rims, wear of tyres, valves.

CHAINS. Excessive wear, cracked or broken rollers, joints, tension.

ENGINE. Oil leaks, compression leaks, main bearings, valves, valve end-caps, valve guides and tappets or push-rods, overhead valve rockers, valve springs, valve seats and faces, split collets, condition of cylinder bore, piston, piston rings, circlips, play in big-end and small-end bearings, timing wheels, shafts and bearings, cams, cleanliness of oilways, sump filter, oil pump, etc.

GEARS. Condition of teeth on sprockets and pinions, damaged ball races, and loose parts generally. Do not forget the kick-starter and foot gear-change mechanism on the Burman gearbox.

The examination should also include all control rods and cables, the plating, clutch and brake linings, S.G. of battery, etc. To sum up, everything should be dismantled, cleaned, and readjusted. If you require some replacement and are not quite

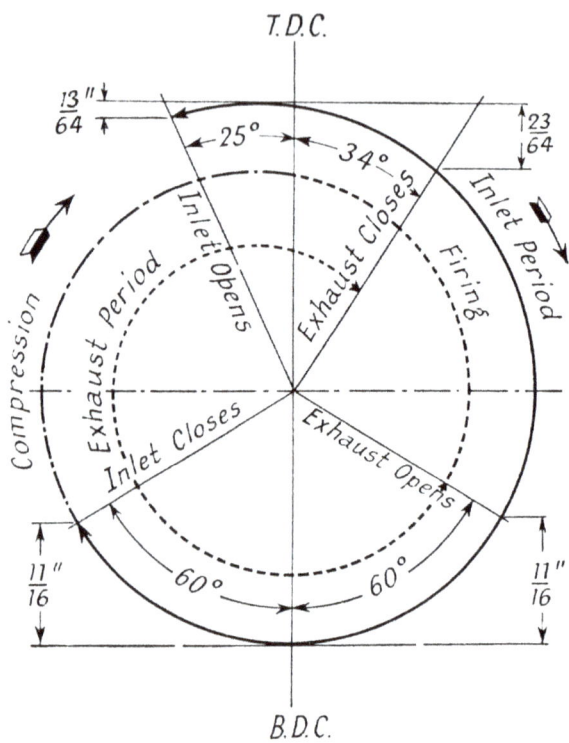

FIG. 38. VALVE TIMING DIAGRAM FOR 1954-8 348 c.c. PANTHER ENGINES

Owners of all earlier 350 c.c. models should refer to the valve timing diagram on page 69

sure what to ask for, send or take the old part to a spares dealer, or else get an illustrated spares list and identify the part.

Dismantling and Assembling Timing Gear (Pre-1949). The cover carries on its inside face two phosphor-bronze bushes, and a spring-loaded bearing cap. This cap presses against the intermediate timing wheel (see Fig. 22) lying between the camwheel and the "Maglita" or dynamo driving pinion, and holds the intermediate wheel (which carries the oil pump) fully home on its spigot bearing, which is very necessary to ensure the proper working of the oil pump. Therefore, do not lose this cap, and do not forget to replace it when reassembling. To remove the cam levers, the bearing pin on which they rock must be withdrawn. To facilitate this, the outer end of the pin has a threaded hole into which a ¼ in. bolt may be screwed, and by gently tapping the inside face of a nut left on the outer end of this bolt the bearing pin will come out of the crankcase. This releases the two cam levers *and* a distance washer *behind them*, and on *no* account must this washer be forgotten when reassembling. Also, when reassembling, do not drive the bearing pin too far into the crankcase, as this will cause the cam levers to bind. If the pads on the cam levers where they bed on the cams show signs of wear, new levers should be fitted. The large intermediate toothed wheel carries the oil pump components—a brass plunger, and engaged in this, a small square brass-block (see Fig. 9). When reassembling, it is best to place the square block in the recess in the plunger, seeing that this is as central as possible, with the plunger in position in the timing wheel, and the whole assembly carefully replaced in its bearing (which is in effect the oil pump body). The pin mounted in the crankcase in the centre of this bearing is placed eccentric to give motion to the pump plunger, and it will probably be necessary gradually to rotate the large wheel when replacing it to get the pin to register with the hole through the square block. When remeshing the toothed wheels, care should be taken that the various punch marks correspond to ensure correct timing (see below). During insertion the cam levers must be raised to enable the cams to pass beneath them. Two punch marks will be found on the cam wheel, one of which coincides with a corresponding mark on the main shaft pinion, and one with a mark on the large intermediate wheel.

When replacing the timing-case cover, see that the faces of the self-alining bearings are as square as possible and renew the paper washer if in any way damaged. For 1949-58, see page 98.

Do Not Experiment with Valve Timing. It is extremely unwise ever to experiment with valve timing other than that arranged by the makers and shown in diagrams, Figs. 37, 38. To ensure on reassembling the timing gear the correct timing, it is only necessary to see that the punch marks coincide as mentioned in the preceding paragraph.

To Retime Ignition (Pre-1949). If the Lucas "Maglita" or Miller dynamo has been removed or the gear drive disturbed, it will be necessary to retime the ignition as follows—

Set the piston so that it is at the top of the compression stroke and as near the T.D.C. position as possible. Verify that it is on the compression and not the exhaust stroke by noting whether both valves are fully closed with the normal clearances at the valve rockers, and put the ignition lever on full retard. Then in the case of "Maglita" models remove the timing-case cover and take off the nut holding the armature-driving pinion to the tapered shaft. This pinion can now be brought out of engagement with

FIG. 39. CLOSE-UP OF 1946-8 PANTHER ENGINE

the intermediate wheel and the armature rotated into any desired position. In the case of Miller coil-ignition models remove the screw on the end of the cam and free the cam from the shaft by screwing a $\frac{5}{16}$ in. bolt into the hole. With the ignition lever still on full retard rotate the armature or cam (as the case may be) until the contacts are just breaking. To find the exact point of break, place a cellulose film between the closed contacts and rotate the armature until the paper is just released, and no more, on pulling it gently. In this position the "Maglita" pinion should be meshed with the intermediate wheel and the locknut replaced. Afterwards check the timing again, and the contact-breaker gap. A preferable timing is to put the piston $\frac{11}{32}$ in. or $\frac{5}{16}$ in. before

IN THE GARAGE

T.D.C. on full *advance* in the case of 348 and 248 c.c. engines respectively. The crankshaft degree equivalents are 35 and 33 degrees before T.D.C. respectively. (1949-58; see page 98.)

To Disconnect Valve Lifter (1938-1948). Turn engine by the kick-starter until the exhaust valve is fully open. This can be checked by the lack of resistance on the valve-lifter lever. Unscrew the valve-lifter fitting on the rocker-box, pull up the valve lifter and slip the nipple out of the connexion. (1949-58: see page 93.)

Reassemble in reverse order, turning the engine until the exhaust valve is open to recouple the valve lifter. The end of the valve lifter can be raised above the rocker-box by a wire hook.

Piston Clearances (Pre-1949). On a new engine with alloy piston the correct piston clearances are 0·004 in. at the bottom, 0·007 in. at the top of the skirt, and 0·012 in. at the ring lands. A rebore is usually required when cylinder wear to the extent of 0·004 in.-0·005 in. occurs. (1949-58 pistons: see page 94.)

Defective Air-release Valve. A possible cause of excessive lubrication of the engine (causing blue smoke at the exhaust) is a faulty crankcase air-release valve. This should be taken into consideration before making any adjustment to the oil pressure. The valve (see Fig. 15) is integral with the nut securing the engine sprocket. Inspect the disc for wear and damage, and make sure that it is not being prevented from seating properly by the presence of dirt. See also page 34.

Cleaning the Sparking Plug. It is a good plan to buy (from an accessory dealer) a small wire brush. Every few hundred miles, remove the plug, inspect it, clean its threads and end with the wire brush, brighten up the electrode points with some fine emery cloth, and check and if necessary adjust the gap which should be 0·018 in.-0·022 in. (0·025 in.-0·030 in. with suppressor.)

To clean a K.L.G. or a Lodge type sparking plug, first unscrew the gland nut from the body of the plug, and withdraw the insulated centre electrode. If the electrode insulator is coated with oil or soot, first wash it in petrol or paraffin. Next remove the carbon deposit with fairly coarse emery cloth or glass-paper. Now again wash the insulator as before.

Clean the firing point of the central electrode with fine emery cloth and scrape the plug body clean internally with a knife or wire brush. Finally rinse the body in petrol.

Smear the internal washer lightly with thin oil and check that it is seating properly in the plug body before inserting the centre electrode and reassembling the plug. Be very careful not to tighten the gland nut excessively. When afterwards checking the plug gap (0·018 in. to 0·022 in.) make an adjustment where necessary by bending the earth electrode to or away from the centre electrode. Under no circumstances attempt to bend the centre electrode. Champion plugs are best cleaned on a Champion service unit.

Dismantling Burman Clutch. To remove the clutch plates unscrew the spring adjuster nuts (see Fig. 28) and remove the

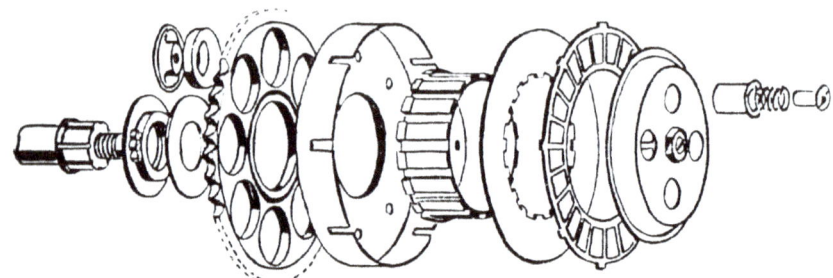

FIG. 40. BURMAN CLUTCH PARTS DISMANTLED
Only one friction and one insert plate are shown above

springs, spring cups, and take off the spring plate, when the other plates may be withdrawn. If desired, the complete clutch assembly may be removed after taking off the spring plate, by unscrewing the nut which holds the clutch body on the castellated mainshaft.

The Sturmey-Archer Clutch (1932-3). The Sturmey-Archer clutches used with the 1932-3 three-speed and four-speed gearboxes are of the single and multiple spring pattern. Dismantling of either type is a comparatively simple matter.

In the case of a single-spring clutch, first unscrew the end cap, using either a special spanner or a hammer and punch. Note should be taken that it has a R.H. thread and must be unscrewed in an anti-clockwise direction. Now unscrew the clutch adjuster nut which is exposed and has also a R.H. thread. The clutch spring and collar can then be removed, allowing the clutch plates to be withdrawn. Be most careful when doing this to note the exact position of each plate so as to ensure their being replaced correctly. If the clutch inserts are thin but otherwise sound, extra spring tension may be obtained by removing one of the washers placed under the clutch adjuster nut. After reassembly be quite sure that the end cap is screwed up thoroughly tight.

With a multi-spring clutch unscrew the six screws which hold the clutch springs and then remove the springs and their boxes.

IN THE GARAGE 75

It is then possible to lift off the spring box plate and withdraw the other plates as in the case of the single-spring clutch. After reassembly it is important to tighten up fully each of the screws holding the springs so as to ensure the springs maintaining an even pressure all round. If this is not done some clutch "drag" may occur.

Rectifying Clutch Slip (Burman Clutch). Clutch slip is most annoying and should be rectified immediately to prevent burning of the clutch inserts. Check over the clutch adjustment and see that there is the requisite clearance of $\frac{1}{32}$ in. between the clutch rod and the ball in the clutch lever (see page 51). Make sure that there is sufficient spring tension and that the spring adjusters are just flush with the clutch end-plate. It should be noted that persistent clutch slip will cause the springs to lose their tension due to overheating. (1949-58 clutches: see page 89.)

Clutch Drag. Sometimes difficulty is experienced in fully disengaging the clutch. This may be caused through wear of the clutch rod, and the remedy is to adjust the adjuster screw and locknut (see Fig. 28) as required. A cable adjustment and/or spring adjustment may also be called for (see page 51) to remedy clutch drag. On oil-bath chain case models clutch drag may arise through the use of an unsuitable lubricant, and the remedy is obvious. Another potential source of clutch drag is the wearing of grooves in the clutch casing by the periphery tongues of the insert plates. The usual cause of this is a worn clutch race which should be renewed, and the offending insert plates and clutch casing also, if badly worn.

If Clutch Springs Unscrew (Burman). On operating the clutch there is a natural tendency for the springs to rotate slightly. This, however, is normally quite insufficient to rotate the spring adjuster nuts. Should the springs adhere to the adjuster nuts through rust or mud, it is possible for the adjusters to turn and thereby reduce the spring tension. The obvious remedy is to clean the adjuster nuts and springs. Also polish the ends of the springs by rubbing on emery cloth, and apply some grease or oil when assembling the springs and nuts.

Looseness of Clutch Sprocket. Movement of the clutch sprocket relatively to the clutch casing is evidence of the shock-absorber rubbers having become worn. The remedy is to renew them. If it is possible to rock the clutch sprocket and clutch casing together without the above relative movement, this indicates that the clutch-sprocket bearing has developed excessive play. If a ball race is fitted, take apart the races and remove one or more of the spacing washers. If a roller bearing is fitted, it is advisable to renew the rollers and perhaps the race itself. With this type of bearing, $\frac{1}{64}$ in. end play is permissible.

Dismantling and Overhauling Gearbox. The author does not advise this being done except by those with a sound mechanical training. Some accuracy in fitting and positioning the components is required and the Panther owner is recommended

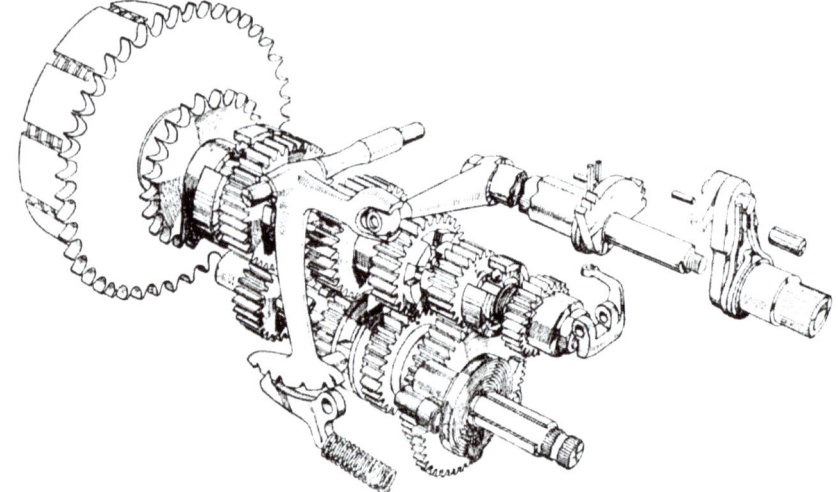

FIG. 41. CONTENTS OF BURMAN FOUR-SPEED "H" GEARBOX

to return his Burman gearbox, if it needs overhauling, to Burman & Sons, Ltd., or to an authorized repairer. ★

Gears Hard to Engage. This is sometimes caused by using an unsuitable gearbox lubricant (see page 35) and the remedy is to replenish with the correct brand and grade. Difficult engagement with a gearbox having foot control may be due to a badly worn ratchet or pawl. In this instance renewal of the worn parts is called for. Other possible causes are an excessively strong pawl spring controlling the gear selector mechanism inside the gearbox, and stiffness of the control joints.

Tendency for Gears to Jump Out. Where hand control is fitted, i.e. on the earlier Red Panthers, this is almost invariably due to incorrect adjustment of the gear control (see page 52). It is also sometimes caused by prolonged wear of the gear dogs or by weakening of the pawl spring controlling the gear selector mechanism inside the gearbox. To cure the trouble, renewal of the parts

★ *Detailed overhaul information for both Sturmey-Archer and Burman gearboxes & clutches can be found in our publication: ISBN 9781588501813*

concerned is required. Where foot gear-change is provided, i.e. on the later P. & C. Red Panthers and on the lightweight P. & M. Panthers, a badly worn foot-control ratchet or pawl may result in the desired gear not properly meshing and jumping out of engagement. Depressing the foot-change lever a second time in an attempt to engage, results in the next gear being engaged, not that originally intended! Remedy: renew worn parts.

Jamming of Kick-starter. Wear of the sharp edges of the ratchet-pinion teeth may cause this undesirable state of affairs. To cure the trouble, file the teeth to a sharp point. If the first tooth on the quadrant is damaged, file this also so as to provide a suitable lead.

Kick-starter Slipping. Possible causes are worn ratchet teeth or a stripped quadrant. Renew the parts affected.

Failure of Foot Change to Return. If the foot-change lever, or the kick-starter lever, fails to return to its original position, immediately suspect a broken or defective spring.

"OLEOMATIC" FRONT FORKS (1947-52)

Very little attention is required in respect of the Panther-Dowty "Oleomatic" front forks fitted to 1947-52 lightweight Panthers. These forks (see Fig. 42) have a combined compressed air and hydraulic damping action, and the Dowty designers (famous for aeroplane undercarriages) state that a mileage of 20,000 can be covered before air requires to be pumped into the fork legs. New forks settle slightly during the first day or so, owing to the oil absorbing some of the air, but such settling is completed before the Panther owner takes delivery of his new mount.

Air Springing and Oil Damping. This combined system used on the Panther-Dowty "Oleomatic" forks has great advantages. The air springing permits of substantial fork deflection when riding over average road irregularities, and at the same time absorbs shocks without the fork movement becoming excessive.

Synthetic rubber cushions moving in oil give constant and equal damping in both directions without the contact and therefore wear of working parts. Should the front forks extend fully, these cushions absorb the shock. Too rapid closing on compression is prevented by the oil cushion between the internal top fittings and the pistons.

The Inflation Valve. This valve (shown at B in Figs. 42, 43) has a special core designed to open at low pressure and provided with oil-resisting rubber seatings. In no circumstances fit an ordinary type tyre valve-insert, as the oil rapidly attacks and destroys seatings made of natural rubber. If a valve core requires

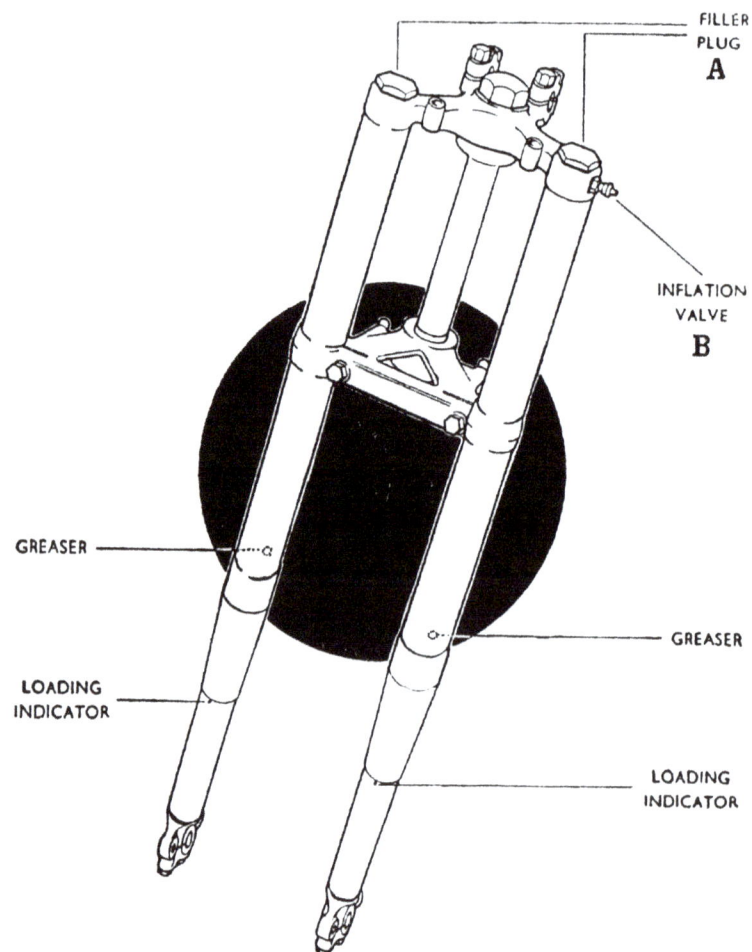

Fig. 42. Sketch of Panther-Dowty "Oleomatic" Front Forks (1947–1952)

The annotations refer to items directly concerned with fork maintenance. Details of the 1953–8 Panther front forks are shown in Fig. 55.

renewal, obtain a new core from a Panther dealer, an accessory firm (see page 83), or direct from Messrs. Dowty Equipment, Ltd., Cheltenham.

To Inflate Forks Correctly. Remove the dust cap from the inflation valve and connect an ordinary cycle pump to the valve.

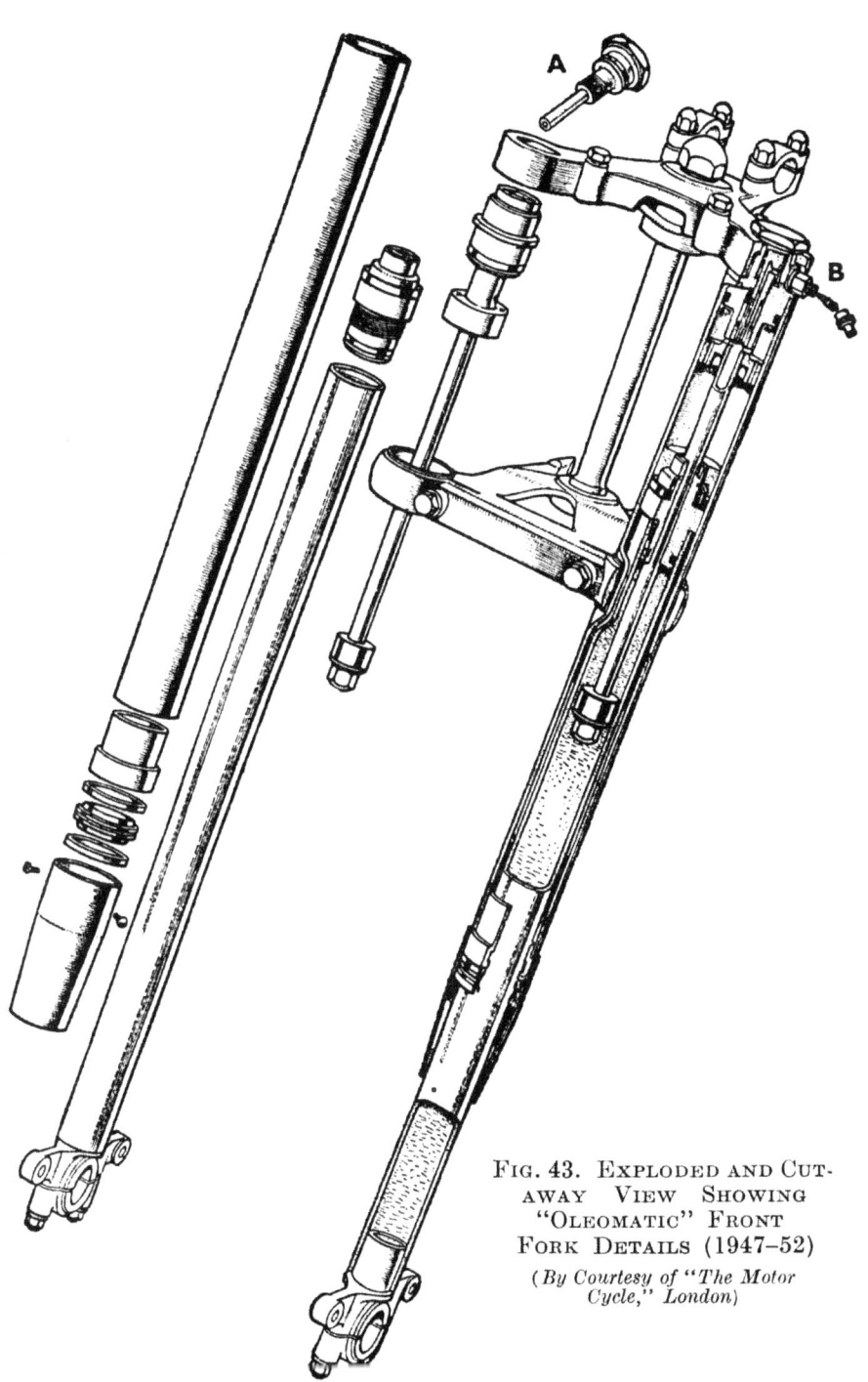

Fig. 43. Exploded and Cut-away View Showing "Oleomatic" Front Fork Details (1947–52)

(*By Courtesy of "The Motor Cycle," London*)

Then over-inflate the front forks slightly by pumping in air. Only a small volume of air is needed. Next sit astride the saddle with the feet on the footrests. To do this with the machine stationary, some convenient support is obviously called for.

Now release air in small amounts by depressing the stem of the inflation valve, until it is observed that *the bottom edges of the shrouds aline with the loading indicators* (see Fig. 42), two red spots located on the front of the two lower sliding-tubes. From the above it is obvious that the front forks can readily be inflated to suit solo, pillion, or sidecar riding.

Topping-up the Forks. Only in the event of "bottoming" occurring with the forks correctly inflated with air is it necessary to top them up. Exercise absolute cleanliness when topping up the front forks, the procedure for which is as follows—

(1) Remove the dust cap from the inflation valve (*B*).

(2) Depress the stem of the inflation valve and permit *all* air to escape. The forks will then close up.

(3) Support the engine crankcase such that both fork legs are *one inch* from the fully closed position.

(4) Remove the two hexagon-headed filler plugs (*A*, Figs. 42, 43) from the tops of the fork legs, and top-up each fork leg with one of the following oils—

   (*a*) Wakefield's Castrolite.
   (*b*) Shell X-100 SAE 20/20W.
   (*c*) Mobiloil Arctic.
   (*d*) Essolube 20.
   (*e*) Energol SAE 20.

(5) Fit and retighten the two filler plugs.

(6) Remove the crankcase support and depress the inflation valve so as to allow all surplus oil to drain off and the forks to close completely.

(7) Inflate the front forks correctly (page 78), according to actual load, and replace the dust cap on the inflation valve.

Refilling Forks. It should *not* be necessary to change the oil in the "Oleomatic" front forks unless (*a*) the forks are stripped right down, (*b*) the oil has for some reason been drained off, or (*c*) the oil has become contaminated during topping-up or filling. If filling becomes necessary, use one of the oils recommended in para. 4 (see above). Follow the procedure already given for topping-up the forks, using, of course, more oil. (2-3 pints.)

Grease Lower Bearings Every 500 Miles. Every 500 miles (or weekly) apply the grease-gun to the two greasers located (see Fig. 42) at the rear of the outer tubes close to the lower bearings.

IN THE GARAGE

Use a good quality grease (see page 37) and inject about two shots through each nipple. Surplus grease will escape through the vent holes provided in the sides of the outer tubes.

Make this Periodical Check. See that the steering-head pad bolt is kept done up tightly, otherwise the alinement of the forks may suffer. Occasionally check also that all nuts and screws are firm.

FIG. 44. CLOSE-UP VIEW OF 1949-58 250 C.C. O.H.V. PANTHER ENGINE (MODEL 65)

The 350 c.c. engine (Model 75) is similar, except that a Lucas magneto replaces the contact-breaker unit

(*By courtesy of "The Motor Cycle," London*)

PANTHER MAINTENANCE (1949 ON)

The foregoing instructions given in this and earlier chapters apply to 1949 and later lightweight Panthers, except where otherwise stated. Appropriate cross-references to this section are included in the earlier text. See also Fig. 52.

On Taking Delivery. If you have been lucky enough to take delivery of a brand new 248 c.c. or 348 c.c. Panther, you should at once check over certain points. First verify that all nuts and bolts are properly tight, and make sure that all attachments are secure. See that the riding position is the best available having regard

82   THE BOOK OF THE PANTHER (LIGHTWEIGHT)

to your physical make-up. Both handlebars and footrests are adjustable and should be moved until the best riding position is obtained. After slackening the handlebar clamping bolts in order

Fig. 45. Close-up View of 1949-58 350 c.c. O.H.V. Panther Engine (Model 75)
Cleanliness of design is a pronounced feature
(*By Courtesy of "Motor Cycling"*)

to make an adjustment, see that they are afterwards firmly re-tightened. If necessary, adjust the handlebar levers.

Can the gear-change lever be operated with the minimum movement of the foot from the right-hand footrest? The lever fits on a splined shaft and full advantage should be taken of this fact.

Is the battery (especially on coil ignition models) well charged, and is the h.t. lead firmly attached to the terminal of the sparking plug? Check these two points by switching on the lamps and pulling on the h.t. lead respectively. Fuel and oil replenishment have already been referred to on page 1.

The Panther Free Service Scheme. If you have just bought a brand new lightweight Panther from a dealer, remember that you

IN THE GARAGE

can take advantage of the Panther free service scheme. The dealer from whom you bought your mount undertakes a single inspection and service free of charge at 500 miles or at the latest three months after you have taken delivery. The only charges made are in respect of materials, grease, and oils.

Detach the free service voucher from the orange coloured leaflet and hand this to your dealer at the time of the inspection. The voucher should be signed and the Model No., engine No. and frame No. included.

Spares and Repairs. When you have occasion to forward or deliver parts to Messrs. Phelon & Moore, Ltd., or an accredited dealer (either as patterns or for repair), it is essential to attach to each part a label bearing your full name and address. To facilitate prompt attention you should keep correspondence and technical queries on *separate* sheets. Always quote the engine or frame number when writing for spares. The registration number of your mount is of no assistance whatever.

In connexion with spares and repairs, it is worth noting that in the London area Claude Rye, Ltd., of 895-921 Fulham Road; Raymond Way, of Willesden Lane, N.W.6; and A. E. Warwick Motor Co., of 236-242 Barking Road, East Ham, E.6, specialize in spares. Jolly & Knott of 128 Lewisham Way, New Cross, S.E. 14, and George Clarke (Motors), Ltd., of 73 New Park Road, S.W.2, handle spares and repairs.

Big firms which generally hold large stocks of spares are: E.S. Motors; The Halford Cycle Co., Ltd.; James Grose, Ltd.; Turner's Stores; Marble Arch Motor Supplies; and George Grose, Ltd. These firms have many branches throughout the United Kingdom and can supply magneto spares, carburettor spares, lubricants of all types, tools, accessories, miscellaneous equipment and clothing. Another good firm is Whitbys of Acton, Ltd.

Tuning Amal Carburettor. Detailed instructions on tuning the carburettor of 1949 and later models are included in Chapter II.

ADJUSTMENTS (1949 ON)

Tappet Adjustment (1949 Onwards). Adjust the inlet and exhaust tappets (clearance *nil* with engine cold) on the 250 c.c. and 350 c.c. engines as described in the last paragraph of page 46.

The Sparking Plug. Suitable types of 14 mm. sparking plugs to fit on the 1949 and later engines are those specified on page 9. For all-weather riding it is an excellent plan to fit a weatherproof terminal to your sparking plug or alternatively to fit a water-tight plug.

Always keep the sparking plug gap correct (0·018 in.–0·022 in.) as described on page 47. For Champion plugs a combined gauge and gap setting tool is available. The cleaning of sparking plugs is referred to on page 48.

Cleaning Lucas Contact-breaker (Models 65, 65 de Luxe). The lubrication of the car type contact-breaker unit is referred to on page 34.

At regular intervals release the two spring clips and detach the moulded cover from the near-side of the contact-breaker unit. Inspect the contacts (see Fig. 46) and see that they are free from

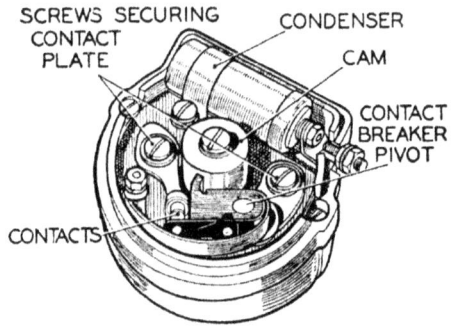

FIG. 46. SHOWING LUCAS CONTACT-BREAKER UNIT AND CONDENSER PROVIDED ON 1949–58 COIL-IGNITION MODELS

grease and oil. Should the contacts show signs of blackening or burning, clean them carefully with the aid of a slip of fine carborundum stone. Alternatively, some *fine* emery cloth can be used if a suitable stone is not available. Having cleaned the contacts, wipe them with a clean cloth which has been previously moistened with petrol.

It may be necessary to remove the arm carrying the moving contact, if the condition of the contacts is very poor due to neglect. To remove the contacts, first unscrew the nut which secures the edge of the contact-breaker spring. Remove the nut and its spring washer. Next withdraw the metal bush and lift the contact-breaker lever from its bearing.

After cleaning the contacts in the manner described above, reassemble in the reverse order of dismantling. Then check the gap between the contacts as described in the next paragraph, and replace the contact-breaker cover which must be clean inside and out.

Checking Contact-breaker Gap (Models 65, 65 de Luxe). An actual adjustment of the contacts should seldom be required. To check the gap (say every 3000 miles), remove the moulded cover

IN THE GARAGE

from the contact-breaker, rotate the engine slowly by hand until the contacts are wide open. Then insert the feeler gauge of the contact-breaker spanner between the contacts (Fig. 46). The gauge (0·010 in.–0·012 in.) should be just a nice sliding fit.

To Adjust Contact-breaker Gap (Models 65, 65 de Luxe). Do not alter the gap unless it varies considerably from 0·010 in.–0·012 in. To adjust the gap, where this is deemed necessary, first see that the contacts are wide open. Next loosen the stationary-contact plate-securing screws (see Fig. 46) until it is just possible to alter the position of the plate. Then adjust the plate position until the gap is 0·014 in.–0·016 in., as shown by the contact-breaker spanner. Afterwards retighten the two securing screws holding the stationary-contact plate, and again check the gap between the contacts. Finally replace the moulded cover on the contact-breaker. When doing this it is important to see that the hinged spring-blade in the contact-breaker makes good electrical contact with the condenser case. Such contact (firm pressure) is necessary to obviate the risk of sparking and burning of the fixed and moving contacts.

Cleaning Lucas Contact-breaker (Model 75). The lubrication of the ring-cam type contact-breaker of the Lucas type magneto is dealt with on page 34.

From time to time (preferably at regular intervals) remove the contact-breaker cover and inspect the condition of the contact-breaker. The contact-breaker, especially the contacts themselves, must *never* be allowed to become oily or dirty. Should this happen, ignition trouble is extremely probable and the contacts will rapidly become pitted and burned. Whenever the gap between the contacts is checked it is desirable to inspect the contacts. Any necessary cleaning of the contacts should be done *before* the gap is adjusted.

Healthy contacts have a grey, frosted appearance. If the contacts are only slightly discoloured, clean both contacts with a cloth moistened with petrol. Should the contacts be found to be blackened, pitted, or uneven, clean them carefully and thoroughly with a *fine* carborundum stone, or should a stone not be available, with some *fine* emery cloth. Having cleaned the contacts, see that all dirt and metallic dust are completely removed by means of a petrol-moistened cloth.

When cleaning and dressing the contacts, do not remove more than the minimum amount of metal to ensure the following—

(1) Brightness of the contact faces.
(2) Perfect truth and smoothness of the faces.
(3) Parallelism of the contacts.

To be sure of obtaining the above conditions, it is best to withdraw the contact-breaker from its housing by unscrewing the contact-breaker securing screw (see Fig. 47). Then pull the complete contact-breaker off the tapered end of the Lucas type magneto armature-shaft. To render the contacts accessible for cleaning, push aside the locating spring and prise the rocker-arm off its bearing.

On replacing the contact-breaker, make sure that the projecting key on the contact-breaker base (the tapered portion) engages the

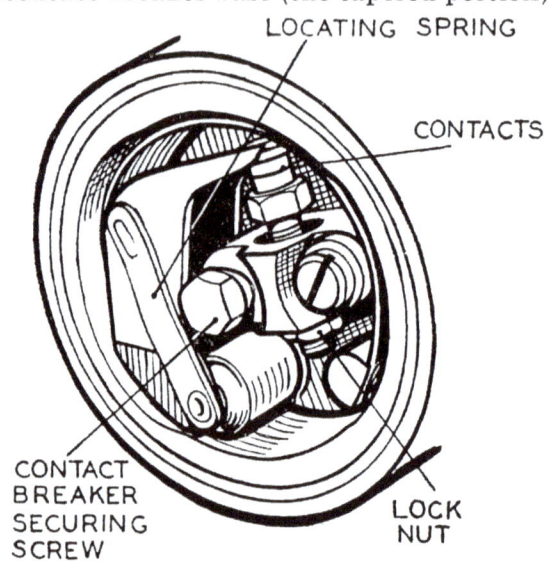

FIG. 47. THE RING-CAM CONTACT-BREAKER OF THE LUCAS MAGNETO FITTED TO MODEL 75

This contact-breaker is of completely different design to that provided on the coil-ignition models, the whole contact-breaker rotating instead of the cam only which in this case is stationary

key-way cut on the armature shaft. Unless this engagement is obtained the timing of the magneto will not be correct. Be very careful when tightening the contact-breaker securing screw. On no account use a long spanner and avoid excessive tightening or slackness. Check the gap after cleaning.

To Adjust the Contact-breaker Gap (Model 75). On the magneto ignition model under normal circumstances it is sufficient to check the gap between the contacts of the contact-breaker once every 3000 miles. If the contact-breaker or the magneto is brand new, however, some initial bedding down occurs, and it is advisable to check the gap after running 100 miles and again after covering 500 miles. The correct gap is 0·012 in.–0·015 in., as checked with

IN THE GARAGE

the feeler gauge of the contact-breaker spanner. Always maintain the gap correct, but do not make an adjustment unless the gap varies considerably from the correct one.

It should be borne in mind that incorrect ignition-timing can be caused if the gap differs considerably from the correct setting. Furthermore, some strain is imposed on the magneto windings. The following is the correct method of checking and adjusting the Lucas magneto contact-breaker gap—

(1) Withdraw the cover from the magneto contact-breaker and slowly turn the engine forwards until the contacts are fully open, with the piston approaching T.D.C. on the compression stroke.

(2) Enter the feeler gauge (attached to the contact-breaker spanner) between the contacts.

(3) If the blade of the gauge just slides in with no appreciable friction, the contact-breaker gap is correct, and no adjustment is called for. If the blade enters loosely, or the contacts have to be sprung apart to permit the blade to enter, adjust the contact-breaker gap as described below.

(4) With the contact-breaker spanner slacken the nut securing the fixed contact (see Fig. 47), and then adjust its screw by means of its hexagon head until the gap between the fixed and movable contacts is found to be correct.

(5) Tighten the locknut securing the fixed contact screw, and again check the contact-breaker gap. If the gap is correct, replace the contact-breaker cover. See that it is quite clean inside and outside.

It will be observed from the foregoing instructions that cleaning the contact-breaker and adjusting the gap between the contacts does *not* require the complete removal of the contact-breaker from the Lucas magneto.

Clean Slip-ring Occasionally. Moisture, dirt, or oil collecting on the slip-ring is liable to cause difficult starting and/or misfiring. About every 2000-3000 miles it is advisable to remove the h.t. pick-up from the Lucas magneto and thoroughly clean the flanges and track of the slip-ring. A practical method of doing this is to wrap a soft cloth around a pencil and press the pencil and cloth against the slip-ring while slowly turning the engine.

The Magneto Pick-up. When you are cleaning the slip-ring also wipe the moulding of the pick-up and polish it with a soft, dry cloth. Visually inspect the moulding for cracks, and scrutinize the carbon pick-up brush and spring. Be careful not to stretch the spring which is somewhat delicate. Renew the carbon brush if it appears to be badly worn. Good electrical contact is essential.

Before you replace the pick-up on the magneto, make certain

that the carbon brush moves freely in its holder and that it beds down properly on the slip-ring track.

Automatic Ignition Advance. On 1949-54 250 c.c. and 1949-54 350 c.c. engines no manual control of the ignition is provided, an automatic ignition-advance mechanism being incorporated in the driving gear (inside the timing case) for the Lucas magneto (or in the contact-breaker unit on coil-ignition models). It is of the centrifugal type shown in Fig. 48, made to Panther requirements.

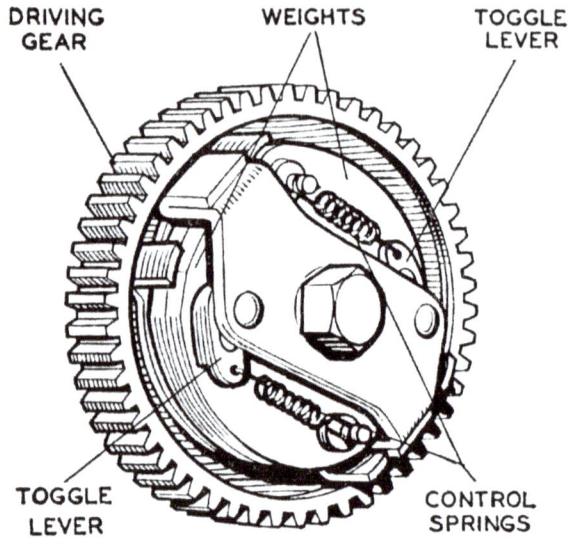

Fig. 48. Lucas Automatic Timing Control (1949-54)

On Model 75, the arrangement is similar to that shown, except for slight modifications to meet Panther requirements, but on 1949-54 Models 65, 65 de Luxe the timing control is embodied in the contact-breaker unit

When the magneto (or contact-breaker on coil-ignition models) is stationary the weights are in the closed position and the ignition is retarded for starting purposes. As the r.p.m. increase, however, the centrifugal force of the weights overcomes the resistance of the control springs and the weights move outwards, causing relative movement between the driving gear and the shaft to which it is fitted. This causes the ignition timing to be advanced with increase in engine speed.

No adjustment is necessary or possible on magneto-ignition models, but on coil-ignition models the rotor can be rotated in the adaptor for the contact-breaker unit. It is seldom necessary, however, to make this adjustment.

Care of Coil. On 1949-58 Model 65 and the 1950-3 Model 65 de Luxe inspect the coil occasionally. Verify that its cap and the

IN THE GARAGE

h.t. lead are quite free from dirt, oil, and moisture. Check for tightness the clamp holding the coil to the frame and also see that the terminals are done up tightly.

Burman Clutch Adjustment (1949 On). Cork or Neoprene inserts are used on the friction plates of the multi-plate Burman RP three-speed or Burman CP or B52 (1955-8 Model 75) four-speed gearboxes provided on 1949-58 Panthers.

Clutch slip (accompanied by engine racing and hot plates) is generally caused by faulty adjustment of the clutch spring adjuster-nuts and/or insufficient free movement in the clutch control, generally the latter. On fabric type clutches it can also be caused by oil or water getting on the friction inserts. The remedy in this case is to remove the plates and clean the inserts with petrol.

As regards the clutch spring adjuster-nuts, always keep the four sleeve nuts screwed up so that their heads are *just flush with the spring plate* (see page 51). During the running-in period some bedding-down of the clutch plates generally calls for periodical clutch adjustment to prevent clutch slip.

The normal adjustment for the Burman clutch is by using a spanner on the cable adjuster. On Model 65 an adjuster screw (*H* in Fig. 28) is also provided (1949-52) in the centre of the spring plate, but this does not apply to the four-speed models. A sticking clutch (usually due to wear of the clutch rod) can generally be rectified by an appropriate cable adjustment.

Unless some free movement is maintained at the handlebar lever, the clutch will almost certainly slip and cause the friction inserts to become burned and need renewing. See that the clutch control cable is free in its casing and that the clutch lever works quite freely.

The Transmission Shock-absorber. All 1949 and later Panthers have a spring-cam type shock-absorber incorporated on the driving side engine main-shaft. This is automatically lubricated and it requires *no* adjustment.

In addition to having an engine shaft shock-absorber, Models 65, 65 de Luxe, and Model 75, have rubber shock-absorbers included in the Burman clutch. They are of the same type as used on earlier Panthers, and as has been mentioned on page 52, renewal of the rubber discs may be necessary after a very big mileage.

To Retension Primary Chain (1949 Onwards). The primary chain, being enclosed in an oil-bath chain case, stretches very slowly. Nevertheless, it is advisable at intervals of several thousand miles to check the chain tension. Note the remarks on page 53.

Turn the engine over slowly and check the tension for every few inches of the chain run, making the check mid-way between the chain sprockets. It is not essential to remove the outer half of the oil-bath chain case, as the fingers can be slipped through the hole uncovered by removing the inspection cap. The correct whip is ⅜ in. to ½ in. and there must be a minimum up and down movement of ⅜ in. all round the chain. Therefore see that a minimum total of ⅜ in. is present with the chain in its tightest position.

To retension the primary chain (all models) it is necessary to pivot the Burman gearbox about its bottom mounting. First

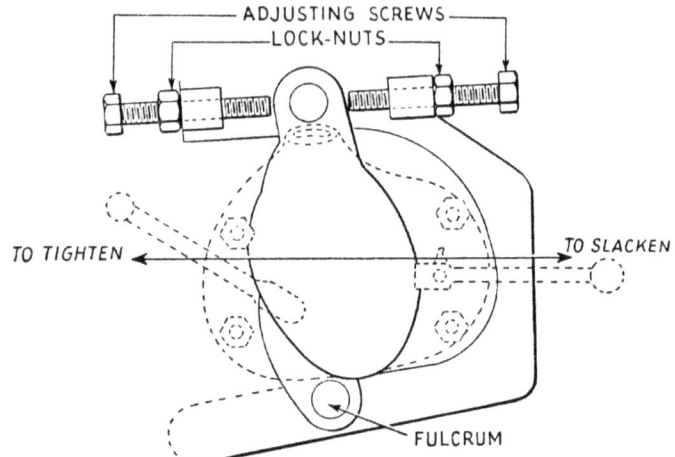

Fig. 49. Method of Tensioning Primary Chain (1949 on)

The Burman gearbox is pivoted about the fulcrum by the two adjusting screws

slacken the nuts on the top and bottom mounting-bolts. Next, unscrew the locknuts on the two adjusting screws (see Fig. 49), which are located on top of the gearbox below the mounting for the battery. Then to take up slackness in the chain, move the gearbox *backwards*. To do this, unscrew the rear adjusting screw a number of turns and then screw home the front adjusting screw until the chain tension is found to be correct. Afterwards screw in the rear adjusting screw so as to secure the gearbox in its new position. Finally, retighten all the locknuts.

To Retension Secondary Chain (1949 Onwards). Eccentric cams (ensuring permanent wheel alinement) are provided for adjusting the chain tension (½ in.–¾ in. whip is correct), and the appropriate instructions (for rigid-frame models) are on page 54. Fig. 30, by the way, shows a slot in the end of the spindle, but this now has a *squared end for spanner application.*

IN THE GARAGE

On 1953 and subsequent models with "swinging arm" rear suspension, when retensioning the secondary chain, place the machine on its central stand (with the rear wheel in its *lowest* position). Then after loosening the hub-spindle nuts, turn the spindle by means of its squared end (on the off-side) until the eccentric cams push the wheel backwards in the fork ends the required amount. There should be a total up-and-down movement in the centre of the chain lower run of $\frac{1}{2}$ in.–$\frac{3}{4}$ in., with the chain in its tightest position.

The Wheel Bearings. All 1949 and later Panthers have large diameter journal-type ball bearings for both wheels. As in the case of the 1945-8 models, these bearings are non-adjustable and should require no attention other than lubrication (see page 38) until many thousands of miles have been covered.

To Remove Front Wheel (1949 On). On all Panthers with Panther-Dowty "Oleomatic" or Panther-type front forks, to remove the front wheel first place suitable packing under the engine crankcase or frame so that the front wheel is lifted clear of the ground, with both fork legs *fully extended*. Next disconnect the front brake operating-cable from the brake cam actuating lever. Also remove the brake anchor plate fixing-screw.

Now loosen on the *brake drum side* the nuts holding the wheel spindle securing-cap. Unscrew the front-wheel spindle nut (on the same side) about *two complete turns*. Take off both spindle securing-caps and ease the front wheel out of the forks, supporting the wheel as it comes clear of the fork legs.

Replacing Front Wheel (1949 On). On Panthers with Panther-Dowty "Oleomatic" or Panther-type front forks, replace the front wheel in the following manner. With suitable packing still supporting the crankcase or frame, place the front wheel assembly in position. Then tighten *fingertight* the four nuts securing the caps which retain the front-wheel spindle (see Figs. 43, 55). On the *brake drum side* tighten the front-wheel spindle nut so that the wheel is firmly held in contact with the side of the wheel spindle fitting. Next tighten firmly the nuts securing the front wheel spindle-retaining cap on the brake drum side (the off-side).

Raise your Panther clear of the packing inserted below the frame or crankcase and "bounce" the telescopic forks several times on the ground. Afterwards tighten the nuts securing the front-wheel spindle retaining-cap on the near side. Finally fit the front brake anchor-plate screw and adjust the front-brake cable (see Fig. 50).

The purpose of the "bouncing" referred to in the previous

paragraph is to make sure that the lower tubes of the fork legs slide quite freely in the outer tubes. A small clearance is provided for this purpose between the shoulder on the near-side spindle ferrule and the spindle fitting.

If Your Panther Has Been Idle for Long (1949-52). Possibly the "Oleomatic" front forks have become deflated owing to the oil seals having become dry. On attempting to re-inflate the forks it may be found that the air is not held. Should this be the case, remove the two filler plugs (*A*, Figs. 42, 43), replenish each fork

FIG. 50. THE LIGHT-ALLOY FRONT HUB AND BRAKE ASSEMBLY (STANDARD 1955-8, MODEL 75; EXTRA, MODEL 65)

leg with a little fresh oil (see page 80), replace the two filler plugs, and proceed to inflate the front forks as described on page 78. After doing this "bounce" the forks several times in a vigorous manner so as to spread the oil. If the above procedure is followed, the forks will afterwards remain inflated.

Tyre Repairs. Should a tyre become "holed" by a flint, nail, or other objectionable article, refer to the advice given on page 55 if you are not already proficient in repairing punctures.

Brake Adjustment. On 1949 and later Panthers, screw adjustment is provided on the off-side for the front forks, and finger-type adjustment is included for the rear brake, a knurled nut being fitted to the end of the brake rod. Note the remarks on page 56 concerning harsh and new brake linings.

IN THE GARAGE

To Adjust Steering Head (1947-58). Where Panther or "Oleomatic" front forks are fitted, loosen the two clamping bolts on the front of the fork-crown fitting, the pad bolt located on the handlebar-clip lug. Then adjust the steering-head nut as required until the front forks are quite free to turn but have no up and down movement in the head. After making the necessary adjustment, retighten firmly the pad bolt and the two clamping bolts. Shown in Figs. 43 and 55.

Care of Dowty "Oleomatic" Front Forks (1947-52). Full maintenance instructions are given on page 77, and this advice should be carefully followed.

Care of Panther-type Front Forks (1953 On). For maintenance instructions applicable to the Panther telescopic forks (which superseded the Panther-Dowty "Oleomatic" type in 1953), see page 102.

Maintenance of Rear Suspension. The lubrication of the "swinging arm" pivots is referred to on page 38. For instructions on topping-up the 1953 Panther-type rear-suspension units, see page 105. As mentioned on page 105, the Armstrong rear-suspension units fitted to 1954 and later Panthers require no maintenance.

DECARBONIZING (1949 ON)

As has been stated on page 57, decarbonizing is normally advised about every 4000-5000 miles, or whenever the symptoms referred to on page 57 become manifest.

Getting Ready for the Job. Note the hints given under this heading on page 57, and see that the engine is thoroughly cleaned down with paraffin before commencing to strip it.

Remove Petrol Tank. Disconnect the petrol pipes and remove the petrol tank by unscrewing the front and rear fixing-bolts. Be careful not to lose the rubber insulation-buffers, metal washers, and split-pins.

"Clearing the Deck." As mentioned on page 58 under this heading, remove the exhaust pipe, carburettor, and sparking plug. Also remove the oil feed-pipe from the crankcase to the cylinder head. With the kick-starter rotate the engine until the exhaust valve opens. Then unhook the exhaust-valve lifter control cable from the lever on the rocker-box. Now turn the engine over until both valves are closed with the piston at top dead centre.

To Remove Cylinder Head and Rocker-box (1949 On). Proceed in the following manner (Models 65, 65 de Luxe, and 75). Remove the rocker-box cover securing screws and withdraw the cover from the rocker-box which is integral with the cylinder head. Be careful not to damage the packing washer placed between the cover and rocker-box. If the washer is damaged, renew it. Next unscrew the nuts which hold the rocker spindles and take out the two spindles. Then withdraw the overhead rockers and also the two push-rods. It is important to keep each push-rod and its corresponding rocker together; therefore be careful not to mix them up. Place them apart in a box pending the reassembly of the engine. Note position of *long* screw for rocker-box cover.

Remove the push-rod cover tubes. Be careful not to damage the synthetic-rubber seals when doing this. Next unscrew the four nuts which secure the cylinder-head to the cylinder barrel. Also remove the bolts securing the cylinder-head stay. Then carefully withdraw the combined cylinder head and rocker-box from the top face of the cylinder barrel. Do not prise the head off, or you may damage the copper cylinder-head gasket.

Drawing Off Cylinder Barrel (1949 On). The engine manufacturers do not recommend too frequent or unnecessary removal of the cylinder barrel. Unless compression is poor and it is desired to inspect the piston rings, it is best not to disturb the cylinder barrel and it is only necessary to scrape the carbon deposits from the crown of the piston and from the combustion chamber, using a *blunt* instrument such as a screwdriver.

If you wish to withdraw the cylinder barrel from the crankcase proceed as described on page 60.

Piston Removal. To remove the aluminium-alloy piston from the connecting-rod, follow the advice given on page 60, and do not forget to *renew the circlips*. On 1949-58 engines the gudgeon-pin clearance in the small-end bush of the connecting-rod is 0·001 in. (maximum). As regards piston clearances, the (new) piston clearances for the *top land* are 0·012 in., and 0·014 in. for 250 c.c. and 350 c.c. engines respectively. At the bottom of the skirt the corresponding clearances are 0·002 in. and 0·005 in. (See page 62.)

Dealing With a Stiff Gudgeon-pin. On a new engine, and for a considerable period, the gudgeon-pin is a rather stiff fit in the piston bosses, and considerable care must be taken when removing or fitting the pin. One method is to heat the piston with a cloth dipped in boiling water, and then tap the pin in or out, using a hammer and suitable drift, care being taken to support the piston firmly on the opposite side when tapping the pin. Another method

IN THE GARAGE 95

is to use a tool such as that shown in Fig. 51. Using this tool, the stiffest pin can be removed or fitted with the greatest ease, and it involves no risk of distorting the piston or connecting-rod. The

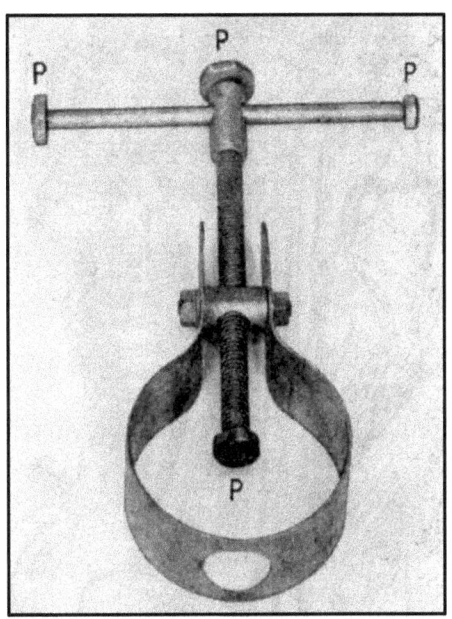

FIG. 51. TERRY TOOL FOR REMOVING AND FITTING GUDGEON-PINS
The metal band is fitted round the piston and the gudgeon-pin pressed
in or out by turning the tommy bar

tool has four pressure-pads P, capable of dealing with all normal size gudgeon-pins.

Removing Carbon Deposits. Note the hints given on pages 62-63. Carbon deposits *inside* the piston, by the way, accumulate slowly and it is seldom necessary to remove such deposits.

To Remove the Valves. All 1949-58 Panther engines have orthodox coil-type valve springs. To compress these duplex springs and remove the split collets, collars, springs, and valves, use the special Panther valve-spring compressor (an extra) in the manner described on pages 63-64. Always scrape the cylinder head thoroughly clean *before* attempting to remove the valves, otherwise there is some risk of the valve seats becoming damaged.

Grinding-in the Valves. Observe the instructions given on pages 64-65. Do not grind-in the valves more often than is necessary

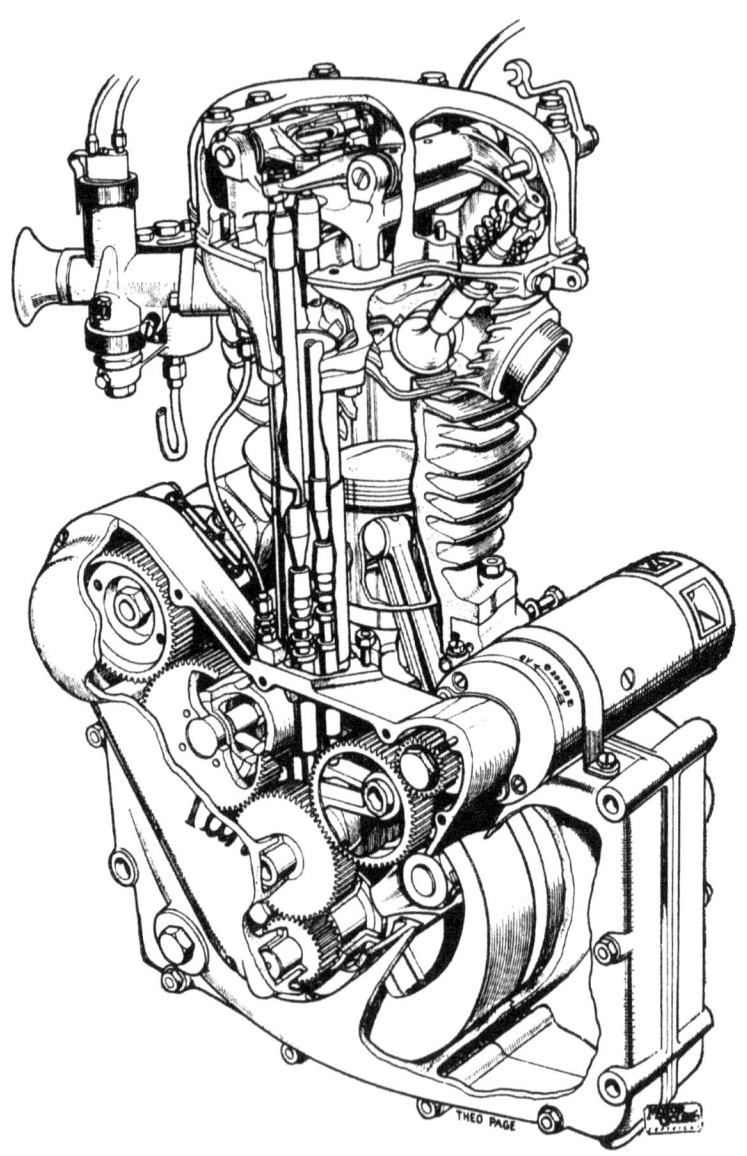

Fig. 52. Partly Sectioned and Exploded View of 350 c.c. Panther Engine (1949 Onwards)

The 250 c.c. Model 65, 65 de Luxe engine is, for practical purposes, the same as the Model 75 engine shown, but the Lucas magneto is replaced by a car-type distributor unit used in conjunction with coil ignition

(*By courtesy of "Motor Cycling"*)

and more than is necessary to obtain a clean face on the valves and seats. On 1949-58 engines no valve stem end-caps are fitted. See that the valves are neither tight nor a sloppy fit in their guides. The minimum clearance of the valve stems in their guides should be 0·004 in.

The Valve Springs (1949 Onwards). Note the remarks on page 65 concerning valve spring renewal. On Models 65 and 75, the *free* length of the inlet and exhaust-valve springs should be $1\frac{3}{16}$ in. for the inner springs, and $2\frac{3}{16}$ in. for the outer springs.* The minimum working length for Panther outer valve springs is $1\frac{7}{32}$ in.

Reassembling the Valves. Do this as described on page 65. It is a good plan to test the valves for leakage after grinding-in and assembling them (see page 65).

Refitting Piston and Cylinder Barrel. Observe the instructions given on pages 66-67. The cylinder-base washer shown in Fig. 36, by the way, does not apply to 1949-58 Panther engines. See that the paper washer is replaced and that it is undamaged.

Refitting Cylinder Head and Rocker-box (1949 Onwards). After grinding-in (where necessary) and replacing and testing the valves, proceed to replace the combined cylinder-head and rocker-box. Clean the copper cylinder-head gasket carefully. If it is at all damaged, renew it immediately. Place the copper cylinder-head gasket on the top face of the cylinder barrel. Then replace the combined cylinder-head and rocker-box, making sure that the gasket beds down properly. Tighten the four cylinder-head securing nuts evenly and in a diagonal order. They must be firmly tightened.

Place in position the push-rod cover tubes, not forgetting the synthetic-rubber oil seals used for the flange joints. Next insert the lower ends of the push-rods in the tappets, being sure that the inlet and exhaust push-rods enter the inlet and exhaust tappets respectively. Replace the two overhead-rockers and their spindles. Tighten the rocker-spindle nuts and before replacing the rocker-box cover, oil the rockers. Then refit the rocker-box cover and tighten its retaining screws. Before fitting the cover make sure that the packing washer is in sound condition. Renew it if damaged, or oil will leak. Fit long screw: centre off-side.

Reconnect the oil feed-pipe from the crankcase to the rocker-box and also the exhaust-valve lifter control cable. To insert the cable in the rocker-box lever, rotate the engine so that the exhaust

---

* On the 1954-8 350 c.c. Model 75 the free length of the outer valve springs should be $2\frac{1}{8}$ in.

valve is open. Fit the cylinder-head stay and be extremely careful not to exert pressure on this in order to fit the two stay bolts. Should the bolt holes not coincide, loosen the locknut and screw in the fork until the length of the stay is such that the two bolts slide in easily.

Clean the Amal carburettor (see page 21), and secure its abutment flange to the flange of the inlet port. Reconnect the exhaust pipe and tighten securely the finned ring-nut which secures the pipe to the exhaust port. Now replace the petrol tank, and see that the control wires passing along the tank are not trapped at any point. Also make sure that the rubber insulation-buffers and washers are in position. Reconnect the petrol pipe and finally check that the tappet adjustment is correct (see page 44).

HINTS ON OVERHAUL (1949 ON)

The Complete Overhaul. Note the advice given in abbreviated form on page 68.

Dismantling Timing Gear (1949 Onwards). Should it be necessary to dismantle the timing gears, no special difficulty should be experienced. A view of the complete assembly is shown in Fig. 52. The following is a brief outline of the procedure to be used.

First remove the two nuts which secure the flange of the lower push-rod cover tube to the crankcase. Pull this tube upwards so that it slides over the upper tube. Next remove the screws securing the timing-case cover and withdraw the cover. Slacken the inlet and exhaust tappets and then take out the camwheel and driving gear. The intermediate wheel (housing the oil pump) can now also be withdrawn.

To remove the oil pump plunger from the intermediate wheel, give it a sharp pull to overcome the oil suction. The remaining gears can readily be removed. Note the following points. The automatic ignition-advance unit (where used), and the contact-breaker unit driving gear on Model 65, must be removed from the *timing case* side. On Model 75, the securing nut for the driving gear serves also as a withdrawal nut, while on Model 65 it is only necessary to remove the split-pin on the end of the contact-breaker unit driving shaft. As regards the dynamo driving pinion, this can be removed *with* the dynamo.

Valve Timing (1949 Onwards). The timing diagram on page 69 applies to 1949-58 250 c.c. and 1949-53 350 c.c. engines. In both cases the inlet valve opens 10 deg. (or $\frac{1}{32}$ in.) before T.D.C. and closes 45 deg. (or $\frac{1}{2}$ in.) after B.D.C. As there is only a single camwheel, the timing can, of course, be checked on the inlet valve only. To ensure correct reassembly, the camwheel and the meshing

IN THE GARAGE

gears are appropriately marked. If the gears are replaced with the markings properly alined, the timing *must* be right, unless serious wear of the teeth has occurred. Fig. 38 shows the correct valve timing for the 1954-8 350 c.c. engines.

Correct Ignition Timing (1949 Onwards).

On the 250 c.c. coil-ignition engines (Models 65 and 65 de Luxe) and the 350 c.c. magneto-ignition engine (Model 75), the correct ignition timing is such that the contact-breaker points are on the point of opening with the piston at T.D.C. (on the compression stroke) and with the ignition *fully retarded*. Always check the contact-breaker gap (see page 84) *before* retiming the ignition or checking the timing.

All 1949-54 Panther engines are fitted with automatic ignition-advance mechanism of the centrifugal type, and when the engine is stationary the ignition is *automatically* fully retarded.

FIG. 53. "BALANCED" DUNLOP TYRE SHOWING CORRECT POSITION OF WHITE SPOTS ON COVER BEAD

Part of the rim is removed to expose the cover bead

Timing the ignition so that the contacts begin to open with the piston at T.D.C., with the ignition fully retarded, gives a maximum ignition advance of 35 deg. before T.D.C. or 0·44 in. before T.D.C. on the piston stroke, (except Model 75) measuring from the top of the cylinder barrel to the top of the piston top land.

To Retime (Coil-ignition Engines).

On 1949 and later 250 c.c. engines with coil ignition, to retime the ignition, put the piston at T.D.C. with ignition fully retarded (see above). Now remove the cover from the contact-breaker unit by releasing the two spring clips. Two cheese-headed screws will be observed inside. Slacken these and adjust the position of the contact between the Tufnol shoe and the cam until the contacts are just on the point of breaking. Afterwards retighten the cheese-headed screws and again check the timing.

To Retime (Magneto-ignition Engines).

On 1949 and subsequent 350 c.c. engines with magneto-ignition, to retime the

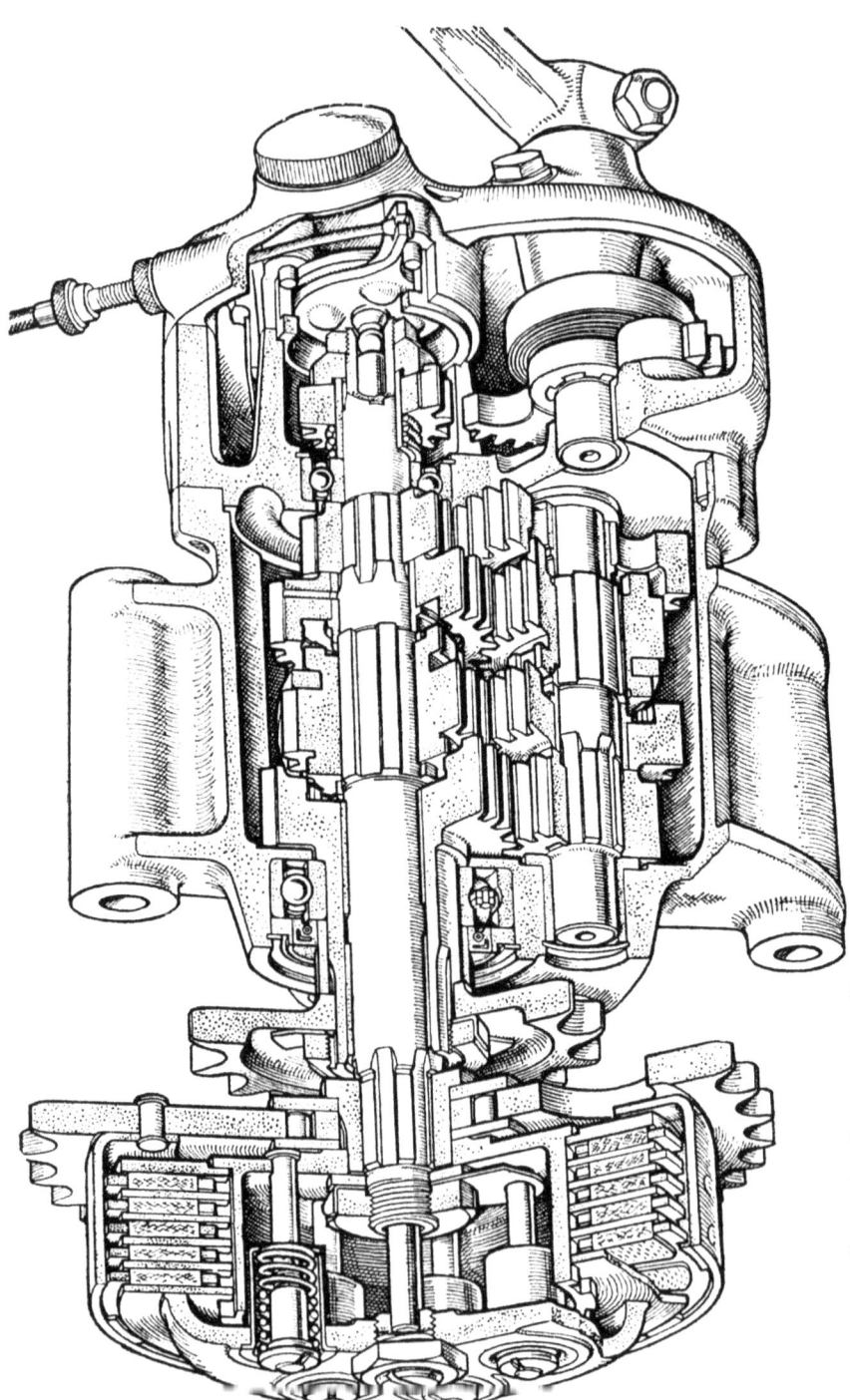

Fig. 54. Sectioned View of Burman Type B52 Four-speed Gearbox and Clutch

IN THE GARAGE

ignition it is necessary to remove the contact-breaker cover and also the timing cover. Next ease the Lucas magneto driving-gear on the magneto armature spindle by unscrewing the centre bolt. This will withdraw the gear from the taper on the end of the armature spindle. Do *not* disengage the driving gear from mesh with the adjacent intermediate-gear housing the oil pump plunger.

Set the piston at T.D.C. and then turn the armature until the magneto contacts are just breaking. This does not apply to the 1955-8 350 c.c. Model 75 with manual control of ignition; on this model fully close (advance) the ignition lever on the handlebars, and set the piston so that it is 40 degrees before T.D.C. (0·59 in. from the top of the cylinder barrel to the top of the piston top land), with the contact-breaker contacts beginning to open. Afterwards retighten the magneto driving gear on the armature spindle, and again check the ignition timing prior to replacing the contact-breaker cover and timing cover.

Timing the ignition so that the "break" commences with the piston at T.D.C. (except 1955-8 Model 75), and ignition automatically fully retarded, gives a maximum ignition-advance on 1949-53 Model 75 of 35 degrees before T.D.C., or 0·50 in. before T.D.C. on the piston stroke, measuring from the top of the cylinder barrel to the top of the piston top land. In the case of the 1954 Model 75 the maximum ignition-advance is as previously stated for the 1949-53 machine.

The Burman Clutch (1949 Onwards). Adjustment of the Burman clutch is dealt with on page 89. Dismantling and other instructions are given on pages 74 and 75.

Overhauling Gearbox. Note the advice given on page 76. Burman gearboxes fitted to 1949-58 Panthers include: type RP (1949-52 250 c.c. three-speed); type CP (1952-8 250 c.c., 1949-54 350 c.c. four-speed); type B52 (1955-8 350 c.c. four-speed). The last-mentioned is a very efficient recent type of gearbox illustrated in Fig. 54.

Tyre Repairs. The subject of tyre repairs is dealt with in some detail on page 55. It should be noted that some Dunlop tyres are "balanced."

If you should find that there is a rubber disc inside the tyre cover, do *not* on any account remove this disc. It is there for balance purposes and does not indicate that the cover has been repaired.

On some tyre covers of Dunlop manufacture, *two white spots* are to be found in the vicinity of the cover bead, and the cover must always be replaced so that the two white spots are close to the valve as shown in Fig. 53.

Care of " Oleomatic " Front Forks. For detailed instructions on the maintenance of the Dowty "Oleomatic" front forks provided on 1947-52 Panthers, see pages 77 to 81.

PANTHER FRONT FORKS (1953 ON)

Very little attention is needed for the Panther-type front forks (see Fig. 55) fitted to all 1953 and subsequent 250 c.c. and 350 c.c. Panthers, and no greasing whatever is needed (see page 37). These forks incorporate normal-type compression springs, and are fully oil-damped. See page 40 regarding 1956-8 forks.

Stiffness Persisting After 5000 Miles. New Panther telescopic forks may seem somewhat stiff for a few thousand miles because of the close-fitting bearings, but normally such stiffness disappears after about 5000 miles when the bearings become quite free. If stiffness persists after about 5000 miles, drain and replenish the Panther forks as described below.

Referring to Fig. 55, remove the drain plug (1), after placing a tray beneath it, from the base of each fork leg. Then work the telescopic fork legs up and down until the whole of the oil in both legs has been drained off.

Insert a box, bricks, or other suitable packing, below the front of the Panther cradle frame, so as to lift the forward end of the machine high enough to enable the front tyre to clear the ground when both fork legs are fully extended. Replace the drain plugs.

Remove the filler plug (2) from the top of each fork leg and through a small funnel replenish each leg with *one-third of a pint* of engine oil (SAE 40). Afterwards, with the fork legs still fully extended, replace the two copper washers (6) and filler plugs (2), and work the telescopic fork legs up and down several times. If stiffness still continues, drain a little oil from each fork leg. Do this after covering a further 100 miles, and be sure to drain off only a small and equal amount of oil from both fork legs. This precaution is essential, otherwise the presence of insufficient damping will cause the forks to "bottom" badly when riding over rough road surfaces.

To Dismantle Panther Forks. First remove the front wheel as described on page 91. Next remove both filler plugs (2) from the upper ends of the fork legs. Also loosen both pinch-bolts in the lower fork-crown. Then withdraw the two fork legs for close inspection. When doing this, be careful not to lose the copper washers (6) fitted below each filler plug and also on top of each fork leg.

To make a more complete examination, now hold the wheel-spindle bearing and with a tommy bar or a special spanner, remove the gland housing (7). The inner tube can now be withdrawn, exposing the upper bearing (8), the lower bearing (9),

IN THE GARAGE

together with the damper-control bush (10). The damper-control spindle (11) is retained in the bottom tube (12). This item should never require renewal because no metal contact should take place. Note that there is a small bleed-hole in the centre tube (13) just above the lower bearing. It is important that this bleed-hole is quite clear.

To remove the upper bearing (8) or the lower bearing (9), unscrew the damper-control bush (10) and withdraw both bearings. Note that the gland housing (7) has a synthetic rubber sealing-ring to prevent loss of oil past the upper bearing. Although this sealing ring is not subjected to high pressures, it is nevertheless advisable to renew it if it has been disturbed. It is only necessary to insert a new ring (circular section) in the gland housing before commencing to assemble the lower tube.

To Assemble Panther Forks.

Thoroughly clean each centre tube (13), thread the gland housing (7), complete with sealing ring on the tube, next the upper bearing (8), the lower bearing (9), and last of all the damper-control bush (10). Tighten the last-mentioned in position.

Clean carefully the inside of the bottom tube (12) and pass it over the bearings, previously smeared with oil; tighten the gland-housing outer tube. This increases the friction on the centre tube. Tighten down firmly, at the same time pushing the tube backwards and forwards to free the gland rubber on the tube. Fit the felt washer in the gland-housing groove and replace

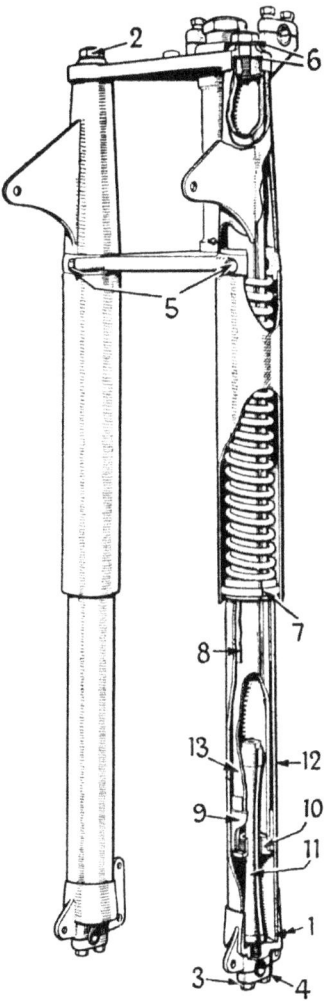

Fig. 55. Cut-away View of Panther-type Front Forks (See also Page 40)

1. Drain plug
2. Filler plug
3. Nuts securing wheel spindle retaining-cap
4. Cap securing wheel spindle
5. Fork crown pinch-bolts
6. Copper washers (two)
7. Gland housing
8. Upper bearing
9. Lower bearing
10. Damper-control bush
11. Damper-control spindle
12. Bottom tube
13. Centre tube

the copper washer (6) on the upper end of the centre tube. Fix it in position by smearing the washer with some oil. Grease the centre tube and pass the spring over it. Then insert the fork leg through the bottom fork-crown into the recess on the upper fork-crown.

A useful draw-bolt can be obtained from the spares department of Phelon & Moore, Ltd., and this tool greatly facilitates the

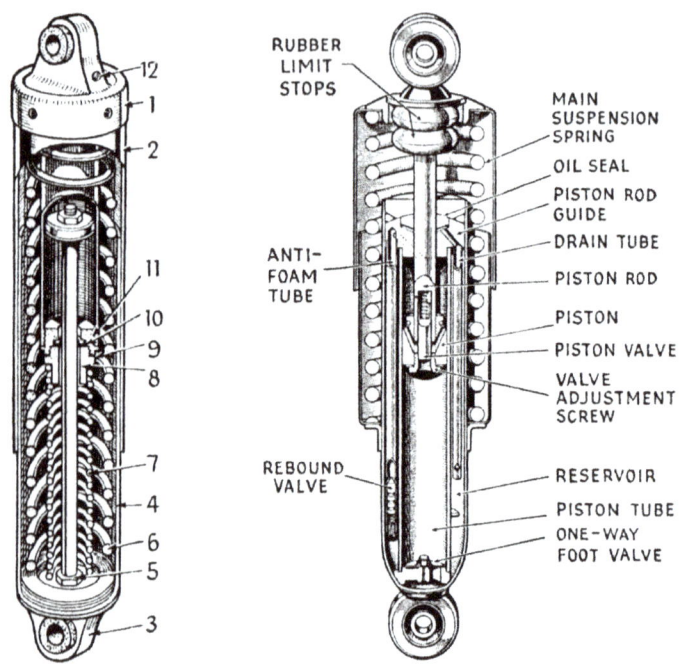

FIG. 56. SHOWING (LEFT) PANTHER AND (RIGHT) ARMSTRONG REAR-SUSPENSION UNITS

The Panther unit was introduced in 1953 and superseded in 1954 by the Armstrong unit

1. Top mounting-lug
2. Outer tube
3. Bottom mounting-lug
4. Bottom tube
5. Piston rod lock-nut
6. Outer spring
7. Inner spring
8. Gland-housing nut
9. Tab-washer for nut 8
10. Gland packing washer
11. Gland housing
12. Plug (one or two)

assembly of the fork legs. To use the tool, pass the draw-bolt through the upper fork-crown, with the draw-bolt nut screwed down on the bolt as far as possible. Then screw the bottom end into the top of the centre tube. Afterwards screw the nut on the draw-bolt against the upper crown and draw the leg against the facing. Prior to removing the tool, tighten the pinch-bolt (5). This will prevent the fork leg slipping back.

IN THE GARAGE

Having positioned both fork legs with the legs fully extended, pour half a pint (250 c.c.) of clean engine oil (SAE 40) into each leg and insert the filler plugs (2). Do not omit to replace the copper washers (6) under the filler-plug heads. Now replace the front wheel (see page 91), remove the packing from beneath the frame and bounce the forks several times with the wheel on the ground.

REAR SUSPENSION (1953 ON)

The Panther Units (1953). New Panther rear-suspension units are charged with sufficient engine oil (38 c.c.) for many thousands of miles running. If after covering 500 miles the suspension units have an excessively free action (causing discomfort), feed some additional SAE 40 engine oil into the oil cylinder of each unit.

Remove both plugs (12) (Fig. 56) from each top mounting-lug, and insert suitable packing under the cradle frame so that both rear-suspension units are fully extended. Then with an oil-can feed oil through either plug hole until it trickles out of the other plug hole. Replace both plugs in each mounting-lug, remove the packing from under the frame, and allow the motor-cycle to rest on the ground in its normal riding position. Now work the frame up, down several times to balance oil on both sides of pistons.

In the event of the Panther suspension units having an excessively stiff action, it is possible to reduce the amount of oil in each cylinder by removing the two plugs (12) (Fig. 56) from each top mounting-lug, and applying downward pressure or weight on the rear of the machine until oil is forced out through the plug holes by the depression of the suspension units. Before getting on the road, verify that all four plugs are replaced and firmly tightened.

The Armstrong Units (1954 On). Details of the Armstrong rear suspension unit are shown in Fig. 56. The oil used in each unit is an SAE 10 mineral oil, and the initial filling is sufficient for an indefinite period. No subsequent topping-up or replenishment is normally required, and no adjustment is needed.

To Adjust "Swinging Arm" Bearing. Straighten the tab-washer. Next turn the outer nut *anti-clockwise* half a turn, and the inner nut *clockwise* until no perceptible end-play is felt. Now turn the outer nut *clockwise* until the two nuts are locked. Again check for end-play. Finally apply pressure to the rear of the machine to confirm that the normal movement of the rear-suspension units is unaffected (by over-tightening of the "swinging arm" bearing). If adjustment is correct, lock the inner nut with the tab-washer.

CHAPTER V
CARE OF LIGHTING SYSTEM (1932-48)

IF you forget all about the lighting system, one dark night it will forget all about you and you may be stranded in a lonely lane with no lamp-post near and no matches in your pocket. This is looking on the "black" side of things and in practice it is seldom that the lighting system gives trouble, provided you pay just that little attention needed. The ignition components of the Lucas "Maglita" and Miller equipment have been dealt with in Chapter IV.

DYNAMO MAINTENANCE

As a general rule, the dynamo gives long and satisfactory service, with practically no attention. There are, however, a few rather important points that should be observed.

Warning. *Before making any adjustments to the headlamp or dynamo, disconnect one or both of the battery terminal connexions.* Failure to do this may incur a burnt-out ammeter or a reversal of the dynamo polarity.

Commutator and Brushes. When in position, each brush should press firmly on the commutator. Periodically the commutator and brushes should be inspected, and all traces of carbon dust and grease should be removed. To clean a blackened or dirty commutator use fine glass-paper. If the commutator has a highly-polished surface (dark bronze colour), leave well alone.

It is advisable to change the brushes before they are worn out, as this will prevent the sparking which gives rise to blackening of the commutator and unsteady charging current, owing to the brushes making imperfect contact. Use only brushes of Miller or Lucas ("Maglita") manufacture for the dynamo. (See also page 115.)

Cut-out. Except for an occasional inspection of the contacts to ensure that these are clean, the cut-out calls for no attention whatever; it should be left untouched except by experts.

Reversed Dynamo Polarity. Should the polarity of the Miller dynamo be accidentally reversed due to touching together or shorting with a spanner the + B. and S.H. dynamo terminals, it is necessary to reverse the battery connexions temporarily, and

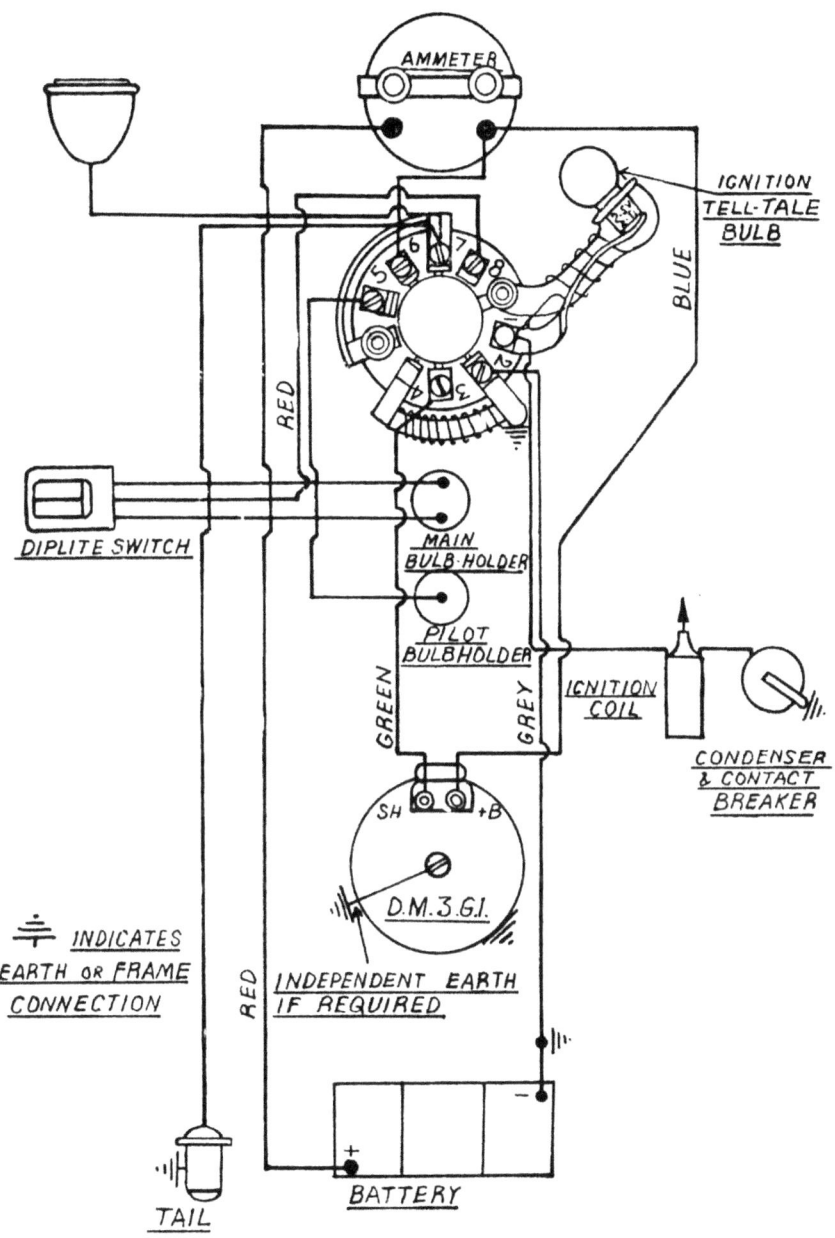

Fig. 57. Wiring Diagram for all Panthers with Miller Lighting and Coil Ignition without Compensated Voltage Control
(H. Miller & Co., Ltd.)

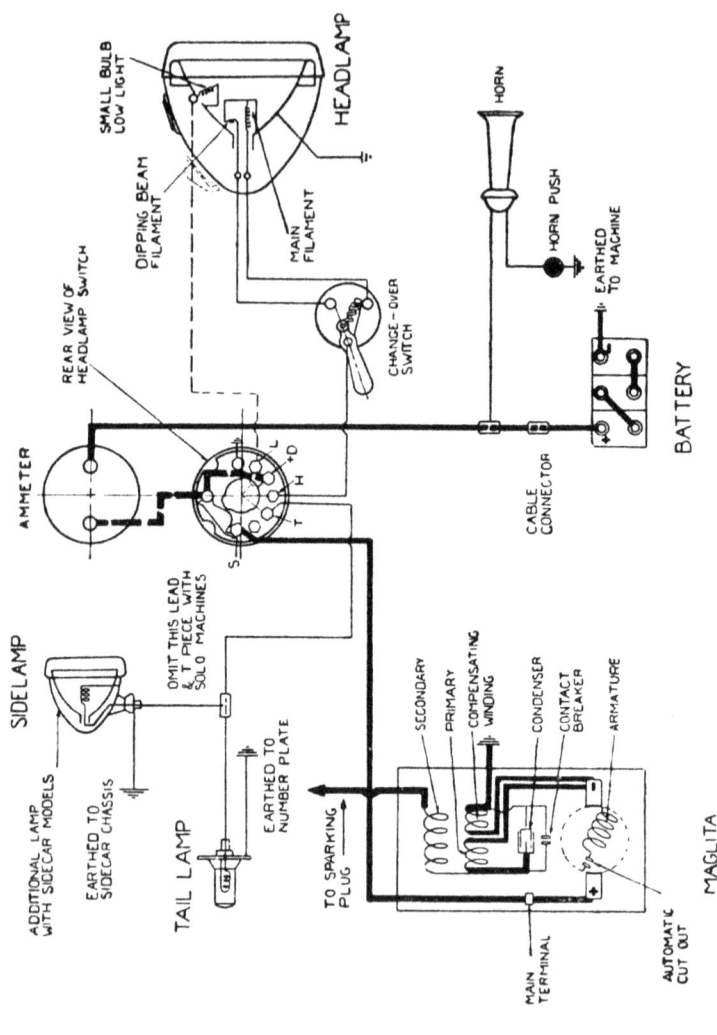

Fig. 58. Wiring Diagram for Red Panthers with Lucas "Maglita" Lighting and Ignition

Internal connexions are shown dotted

(*Joseph Lucas, Ltd.*)

CARE OF LIGHTING SYSTEM (1932-48)

again make contact between the + B. and S.H. terminals, in order to restore the dynamo to normal and obtain a charge. After making contact between the + B. and S.H. terminals, the battery connexions should be changed back again, when on starting up the engine with the switch on "charge," the dynamo will function correctly. The above does not apply to the 1939 Model 40.

Lubrication. This matter is dealt with on page 35. Avoid using too much oil when lubricating the Lucas "Maglita" contact-breaker, or it may reach the contacts and cause trouble.

CARE OF LAMPS (1932-48)

Cleaning Reflectors. Should a reflector be merely dusty, wipe gently with a "Selvyt." Do not use metal polish, as this dulls the surface. Replace a reflector as soon as it becomes very dull, or a great proportion of the lamp illuminating-power will be lost.

Focusing Headlamp. The best way to do this is to take the machine out to a straight, level road; find the correct bulb adjustment; and also verify that the alinement of the headlamp is correct (see page 121). The main driving light should, of course, be switched on when focusing is carried out. Actual focusing is carried out in the following manner. Insert the Miller bulb (see below for type) and when the bayonet pins are right home, exert a further twisting force to the right. This will permit of the bulb and its holder being slid forwards or backwards the necessary amount to obtain proper focus. On removing the additional twisting force the bulb holder is securely locked in position.

Special care should be taken to see that the bulb is in its correct position relative to the reflector.

Bulb Renewals. Always use Miller or Lucas bulbs, except perhaps where the warning lamp bulb is concerned (a 2·5 volt flash-lamp bulb* will do). It is a good plan to carry some spare bulbs in a special bulb carrier. The correct Miller bulb replacements are a 6 V. 18/18 W. gas-filled double-filament S.B.C. main bulb, a 6 V. 3 W. vacuum S.C.C. pilot bulb and a 6 V. 3 W. vacuum tail light bulb. The correct Lucas bulbs are a 6 V. 12/12 W. double-filament main bulb, a 6 V. 3 W. S.C.C. pilot bulb and a 6 V. 3 W. S.C.C. tail-lamp bulb. When fitting new bulbs to the headlamp, be sure to place the "Diplite" bulb the right way round, that is, with the "Diplite" filament *above* the centre filament.

* On 1939 de Luxe Model 40 with compensated voltage control a flash-lamp bulb will not do. Instead, use an 8 volt, 0·1 amp. bulb.

CARE OF BATTERY (1932-48)

If the battery is to maintain its capacity and give satisfactory service, it is absolutely essential to pay regular attention to it. On coil-ignition machines, where current is taken from it both for lighting and ignition, it is doubly important. There are four vital points to remember. These are as follows—
1. Keep the acid level just above the tops of the plates.
2. Add only *distilled* water; never tap water.
3. Occasionally test the condition of the battery by taking specific gravity readings with a hydrometer.
4. Never leave the battery in a discharged condition.

Topping-up. Examine the acid level about every four weeks, and even more frequently in hot weather and tropical climates. Be careful not to hold a naked light near the vent holes. If the level is below the tops of the plates, add distilled water as required. This should be added just before a charge run, as the agitation due to running and the gassing will thoroughly mix the solution. If the solution has been spilled by accident, add diluted sulphuric acid of equal specific gravity to that in the remaining cells. It is desirable occasionally to take hydrometer readings (specific gravity values) of the solution in the cells, as described on page 119. These readings are the most reliable method of indicating accurately the condition of the cells. Keep the battery connexions clean and free from acid. Smear well with petroleum jelly to prevent corrosion.

Battery Removal. In the case of Models 20, 30, topping-up of the battery necessitates disconnecting the short wires leading from the battery and removing the complete battery from the machine, when the lid can be detached and the cells attended to. On the Model 40 Red Panther and the Panther lightweights, however, the battery may be lifted partly out on the off-side of the machine after disconnecting one of the wires. Slacken the wing nuts and remove the right-hand clip. Then take off the battery lid and examine the electrolyte.

Charging Hints (C.V.C. not Fitted). Charging varies according to various running conditions. If the light is poor and falls off when the machine is standing, charging should be immediately carried out. It is difficult to lay down rigid instructions on the question of charging, since it largely depends upon the extent to which the lamps are used. With the coil-ignition models more charging is necessary than with the "Maglita" models, since the current is used for ignition and lighting. The following suggestion

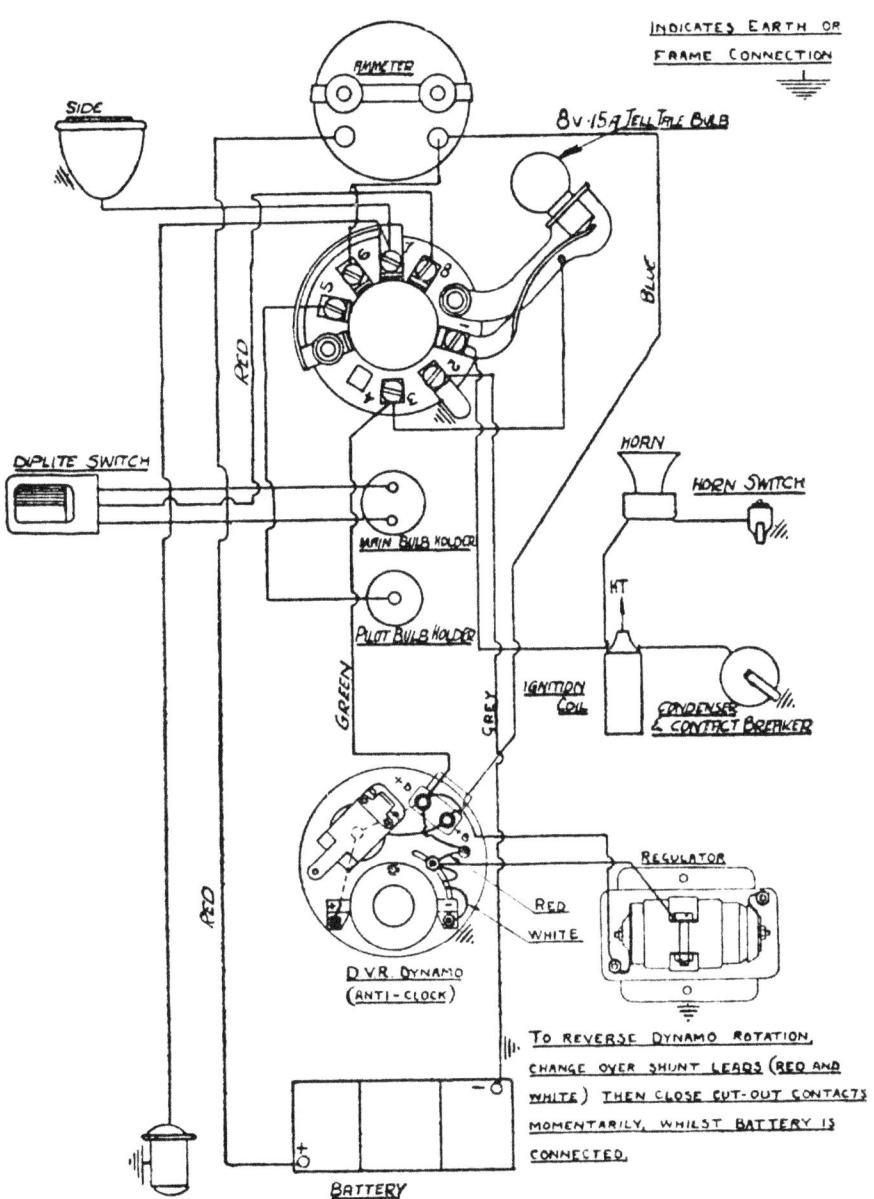

Fig. 59. Wiring Diagram for all Panthers with Miller Dynamo Lighting, Coil Ignition and Compensated Voltage Control
Applicable to the 1939 Model 40
(H. Miller & Co., Ltd.)

may serve as a rough guide: leave the switch in the "charge" position during the day for about 50 per cent of the night riding (a slight charge should flow to the battery when running with lamps on). Charging a battery after discharge raises the specific gravity, and discharging lowers the specific gravity. Place on charge, either by running the engine or using an independent electrical supply, immediately any battery whose specific gravity has fallen as low as 1·210. Take hydrometer readings whenever trouble is experienced with any part of the electrical system. *The correct specific gravity reading is* 1·280–1·300 and 1·260–1·280 in the case of the Lucas and Miller batteries (fully charged at 60° F). See also page 119.

The behaviour of one cell differing from that of the others requires prompt attention and more frequent inspection, especially if the difference increases with time. Should the acid level fall more rapidly in one cell than in any of the others, the container of this cell is probably leaky and needs repairing; again, if the specific gravity of one of the cells is lower than that of the other, and observation reveals that the loss continues, inspect this cell.

Compensated Voltage Control (1939 and Later Models). Do not interfere with the adjustment of the Miller regulator. If trouble arises, return it to the makers. Keep the battery connexions clean and tight, otherwise the ammeter readings will suggest a fully charged battery when such is not the case. Also do not neglect a badly discharged battery. See that the dynamo to regulator cable insulations are sound and that the connexions are good. The earth contact of the regulator must also be perfect.

The regulator (which works on the "trembler" principle) is connected across the dynamo brushes and operates only when the dynamo voltage reaches about 7·3 volts. It controls automatically the dynamo output according to the load on the battery and its state of charge. Daylight readings vary between 1 and 6 amps., according to the battery condition; if it is almost fully charged the regulator will produce a trickle charge of only about 1 amp., and this even if the switch is in the "Off" position. For normal night work a slight charge should show on the ammeter. If the machine is stationary with contacts closed, a discharge of 4 amps. plus a small discharge due to the warning bulb is indicated.

Warning Lamp. A "tell-tale" lamp is mounted close to the ammeter on all coil-ignition models to remind the rider to switch off the ignition when parking the machine (see page 8). It should be noted that the warning lamp lights when the headlamp switch is moved to the "Charge" position and the dynamo is stationary. The lamp goes out as soon as the dynamo functions and the

CARE OF LIGHTING SYSTEM (1932-48)

contacts of the cut-out close. If the lamp remains on, either the cut-out contacts are not closing or else the dynamo itself is not generating a current. A faint glow of the lamp can sometimes be discerned when the dynamo is generating at maximum output.

Coil Maintenance. The coil is a lazy item and as nothing in it moves, wear does not occur. Its sole occupation is the conversion by inductance of a low-tension current into a high-tension current, and it cannot do this without the help of the contact-breaker. Beyond occasionally wiping the insulated terminal-sleeve and terminal cap with a cloth damped in petrol, no maintenance is required. Should the coil become hot at any time, this would suggest a break-down in the internal insulation. Never allow water to get on the coil terminals.

If the Warning Lamp Breaks. This will not interfere with the functioning of the ignition system because the bulb is connected in parallel with a small resistance and both bulb and resistance are connected in series with the coil when the ignition is switched on. However, a broken bulb should be replaced as soon as possible (see page 109).

What to do if the Battery goes " Flat." Do not despair; you can, on a coil-ignition model reach home by rigging up temporarily a medium-size flash-lamp battery (cells connected four in series to give about 4 volts). This expedient should enable the ignition system to function for 20-30 minutes at least. After stopping for about 10 minutes it should be possible to obtain a further 20 minutes' running, and so on until the flash-lamp battery also becomes quite "flat." During such running the dynamo plug must be removed.

If Dynamo Fails to Charge. If no charge is produced by the dynamo, i.e. if the cut-out fails to close and the warning lamp remains bright, the following is the procedure required on 1939 Panther C.V.C. models. Examine the commutator and brushes (see page 106). If these are in serviceable condition, inspect the dynamo to regulator cables and the connexion for the earth contact. Look for frayed insulation. If there is still no visual defect, remove the regulator cartridge from its clips, operate the dynamo and note if a charge is obtained. If this is the case, run the machine temporarily without the regulator cartridge, but at the earliest opportunity fit a new one. On *no* account tamper with the regulator unit. This should be returned to H. Miller & Co., Ltd., Aston Brook Street, Birmingham, 6 for attention, or sent to one of their service agents.

CHAPTER VI

CARE OF LIGHTING SYSTEM (1949 ON)

BY giving routine attention to your lighting system as described in this chapter you should be able to avoid annoying trouble on the road and also obtain the maximum illumination from your lamps. On no account neglect the battery. On coil-ignition models, remember that this supplies current for the ignition system as well as the lights. The components of the ignition system are dealt with in Chapter IV.

The Lucas Equipment. On 1949 and later 250 c.c. and 350 c.c. vertical-engined Panthers (Models 65, 65 de Luxe, and Model 75), Lucas equipment is fitted as standard. A Lucas-type dynamo is strapped on the top of the crankcase at the front and is gear-driven from the camwheel. A compensated voltage control unit (C.V.C.) is strapped to the frame beneath the saddle and automatically takes care of charging the battery.

A Lucas-type 12 amp. hr. lead-acid battery is strapped to a platform over the gearbox and supplies current to the Lucas lamps, electric horn (over front engine plates), and the coil-ignition system (in the case of 250 c.c. engines).

The headlamp is a Lucas type MU42, MCH55 or MCH58 incorporating the lighting switch and centre-zero ammeter. It has a double-filament main bulb, with dimming control by a switch mounted on the left-hand side of the handlebars (see Fig. 1). The rear lamp is a Lucas type MT211. 1955–8 models have Lucas type 525 stop-tail lamps. Wiring diagrams for the 1949 and later equipment are shown on pages 128–132.

DYNAMO MAINTENANCE (1949 ON)

To Avoid "Shortings." Precautions are unnecessary for inspecting the commutator, but on making adjustments to the wiring circuit, it is essential to take steps to prevent accidental "shorting." Disconnect the lead from the lighting switch to the battery *positive* (negative, 1952 on) terminal. Push back the rubber shield; then unscrew the cable connector. Be sure that the cable does not make contact with any metal part of the frame, otherwise a "fat" spark will indicate that the battery *was* well charged! When reconnecting the lead, pull the rubber shield well over the connector.

After a Big Mileage. It is a good plan every 10,000 miles to entrust the dynamo to a Lucas service depot for dismantling,

CARE OF LIGHTING SYSTEM (1949 ON)

cleaning, servicing, and lubrication. Lubrication is referred to on page 35.

Inspect Commutator and Bushgear. The Lucas-type dynamo will run satisfactorily for thousands of miles with scarcely any attention other than occasional inspection of the commutator and brushgear. It is advisable once a season, about every six months, to remove the metal cover from the dynamo and make a careful inspection.

Commutator Brushes (Lucas Dynamo). The brushes must make good electrical contact with the commutator. They must be absolutely clean and able to move freely in their box type holders, on holding back the retaining springs and gently pulling the leads and then releasing them. There must also be perfect contact between the brushes and the copper segments of the commutator; the brush faces in contact with the segments should be uniformly polished. Clean the brushes with a petrol-moistened cloth after removing them. To do this, pull back each brush-retaining spring

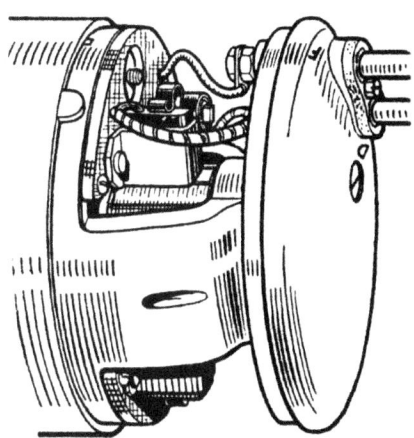

FIG. 60. COMMUTATOR END OF LUCAS DYNAMO FITTED TO MOST PANTHERS

The metal cover is shown removed. Insert some thin machine-oil through the lubricator (where provided) every 4000-5000 miles

(see Fig. 60) and remove the brush by pulling on its lead, being careful to see that the brush pressure spring is clear of the brush holder.

Examine the carbon brushes for wear and unevenness, and true them up if necessary. Generally it is best to replace the brushes *before* serious wear develops, as this prevents sparking, which causes blackening of the commutator and an unsteady charging current.

If Lucas brushes become so badly worn that it is necessary to remove them, this can easily be done as follows: Release the eyelet on the brush lead by unscrewing the hexagonal nut or screw at the terminal; then, holding back the spring lever out of the way, withdraw the brush from its holder. Renew with genuine Lucas brushes.

The brush springs should be inspected occasionally to see that they have sufficient tension to keep the brushes firmly pressed against the commutator surface when the dynamo is running. It is particularly necessary to keep this in mind when the brushes have been in use a long time and are very much worn down.

It is unwise to insert brushes of a grade other than that supplied with the dynamo, or to change the tension springs. The arrangement provided has been made only after many years' experience, and will be found to give the best results and the longest life. It is really best, when the brushes become so worn that they no longer bed down on the commutator, to have new brushes fitted at a Lucas service depot, as this ensures the brushes being properly "bedded."

Care of Commutator (Lucas Dynamo). The surface of the commutator segments should be kept clean and free from oil or brush dust, etc. Should any grease or oil work its way on to the commutator through over-lubrication, it will cause not only sparking, but, in addition, carbon and copper dust will collect in the grooves between the commutator segments.

The best way to clean the commutator is, without disconnecting any leads, to remove from its box-holder one of the main brushes and, inserting a fine duster, hold it, by means of a suitably-shaped piece of wood, against the commutator surface causing the armature to be rotated at the same time. If the commutator has been neglected for long periods, it may need cleaning with fine glasspaper, but this is more difficult to do, and should not be necessary if it has received regular attention. The segments should be *dark bronze* and highly polished.

Lucas Compensated Voltage Control. All 1949 and later Panther motor-cycles incorporate compensated voltage control. The C.V.C. unit consists of a cut-out and voltage regulator unit neatly housed in a box beneath the saddle. The unit is connected between the dynamo and battery and sees to it that the battery is automatically charged the right amount by varying the dynamo output according to the state of charge of the battery and the load imposed on it.

Current is prevented from flowing back from the battery to the dynamo at low r.p.m. by means of the cut-out which opens. As soon as the r.p.m. rise high enough to enable the dynamo to charge the battery, the cut-out closes and completes the circuit.

In all three lighting switch positions (see page 120) the dynamo gives a controlled output and thus relieves you of responsibility in regard to charging. The regulator begins to operate when the dynamo voltage reaches about 7·3 volts. During daylight running with the battery well charged and the switch in the "Off" position, the dynamo gives only a trickle charge, and the ammeter

CARE OF LIGHTING SYSTEM (1949 ON)

reading is unlikely to exceed 1-2 amp. There is no danger of overcharging.

The regulator provides for an increase of dynamo output as soon as the lamps are switched on. The effect of switching the lamps on after a long run with the battery voltage high is often to cause a temporary discharge reading at the ammeter, but fairly soon the voltage falls and the regulator responds, thereby causing the output of the dynamo to balance the load of the lamps.

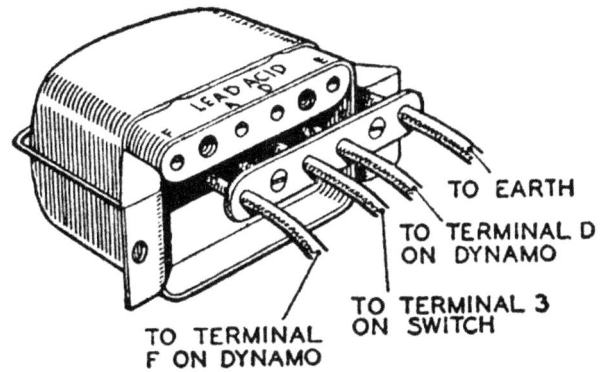

FIG. 61. LUCAS CUT-OUT AND REGULATOR UNIT CONNEXIONS

When the battery is in a discharged state, the regulator increases the dynamo output and restores the battery to its normal state of charge in the shortest possible time.

Do Not Meddle with C.V.C. Unit. The unit is sealed by the makers, as it does not need adjustment once it is correctly set. The only conceivable trouble is oxidizing or welding together of the contacts, owing to accidental crossing of the dynamo field and positive leads. Be careful if making wiring alterations (see page 127). Referring to Fig. 61, make sure that the C.V.C. unit connexions are correct, tight, and that the insulation is sound. See also last paragraph on page 127.

Should you fit a "Lucas-Nife" battery in place of the lead-acid type, you must fit a new regulator to ensure a good charging rate with a discharged battery. You are advised to have the change-over made at a Lucas service depot and to visit a depot whenever any serious electrical fault develops.

BATTERY MAINTENANCE (1949 ON)

Neglect of the Lucas-type 12 amp. hr. lead-acid battery quickly brings trouble, and correct attention in regard to its maintenance is *vitally* important. Upon it depend the lamps and horn.

Examine Acid Level Regularly. About every four weeks, and even more frequently in tropical climates, unscrew the battery clamping nut and remove the battery. Then take off the battery lid and remove the three vent plugs. Inspect the hole in each vent plug and make certain that it is not obstructed. A choked vent

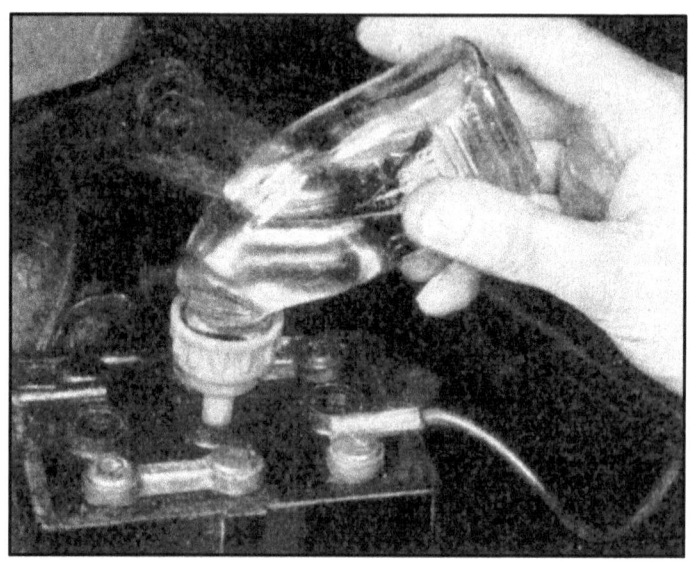

FIG. 62. TOPPING-UP THE BATTERY WITH A LUCAS BATTERY FILLER
Always remove the battery when doing this

plug hole will result in an increase of pressure in the cell owing to "gassing," and this may cause trouble.

Wipe the top of the battery clean with a rag and also verify that the rubber washers (if fitted beneath vent plugs, to prevent leakage), are in position. After wiping the top of the battery, either destroy the rag or wash it thoroughly, using several changes of water. See that a supply of clean distilled water is to hand.

Be careful not to hold a naked light near the vents. If the level is below the tops of the separators, add *distilled* water* as required to bring the electrolyte level with the tops of the plate separators. This should be done just before a charge run with a Lucas battery filler, as the agitation will thoroughly mix the solution. Acid must not be added to the electrolyte unless the solution has been spilled by accident, in which case add diluted sulphuric acid of specific gravity equal to that in the cells.

* The distilled water, unlike the acid, is lost gradually by evaporation. Bottles of distilled water can be obtained from most garages and from chemists.

CARE OF LIGHTING SYSTEM (1949 ON)

Undoubtedly the best way to top-up a Lucas battery of the type shown in Fig. 63, *A*, is to use a Lucas battery filler. Insert its nozzle into each cell with the nozzle resting on the separators. Hold the battery filler in this position until air bubbles cease to rise in the glass container. The electrolyte level should then be correct; examine it to be sure.

On later Panther machines with the Lucas PUZ7E/9 battery, pour distilled water round the flange (not the tube) of the acid-level device (see Fig. 63, *B*) until it stops draining into the cell. Then lift the tube slightly to enable the small amount of water in

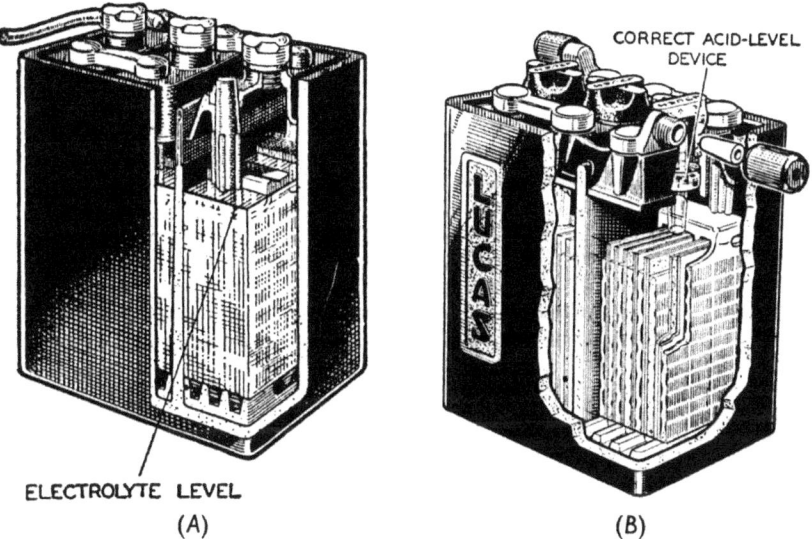

Fig. 63. Keep the Electrolyte Level with the Tops of the Plate Separators

On the left is shown the Lucas battery fitted prior to 1955, and on the right the later PUZ7E/9 battery with correct acid-level device

the flange to drain into the cell. The electrolyte level should then be correct. Inspect to make certain.

If the battery needs to be topped-up very often, it is possible that the C.V.C. unit needs to be adjusted; if one cell requires more frequent topping-up than the others, probably the battery case, or container, is cracked, and battery renewal is called for.

Check Acid Specific Gravity. Occasionally, hydrometer readings (specific gravity values) should be taken of the solution in each of the cells. The method of doing this is not complicated. The Lucas hydrometer contains a graduated float which indicates the specific gravity of the battery cell from which a sample of electrolyte is taken.

After a sample has been taken and checked, it must, of course, be returned to the cell. The taking of S.G. readings with a hydrometer is the most efficient way of ascertaining the state of charge of the battery. The S.G. readings should be approximately the *same for all three cells*. Should the reading for one cell differ substantially from the readings for the others, probably some acid has been spilled or has leaked from the cell concerned. There is also a possibility of a short-circuit between the battery plates. In the latter case it will be necessary to return the battery to a Lucas service depot for attention.

Under no circumstances must the battery be permitted to remain in a discharged condition for long, or serious deterioration will occur. After checking the S.G. readings and topping-up the cells, wipe the top of the battery and remove any spilled electrolyte or water; replace the three vent plugs and the battery lid. Then fit and tighten the battery clamping-screw.

Keep Connexions Clean. Always keep the battery connexions clean, free from corrosion, and tight, otherwise the ammeter readings will *not* indicate the true state of charge of the battery. To prevent corrosion they should be smeared with petroleum jelly.

Correct S.G. Readings. With Lucas batteries fitted to Panther machines, the specific gravity readings at an acid temperature of approximately 60° F. should be: 1·280–1·300, battery fully charged; about 1·210, battery about half discharged; below 1·150, battery fully discharged.

Never leave the battery in a discharged state for any appreciable period. A low state of charge often is caused through parking the machine for long periods with the lighting switch in the "L" position, unaccompanied by much daylight running. The remedy is, of course, to undertake more daylight running and to keep the switch in the "Off" position as much as possible until the battery regains its normal state of charge. If overcharging occurs, have the setting of the compensated voltage control unit checked.

LAMP MAINTENANCE (1949 ON)

The Lighting Switch. The lighting switch (incorporated on a panel on top of the 1949-54 MU42 headlamp or built into the offside on the 1955-8 MCH55 and MCH58 headlamps), being connected in the compensated voltage control circuit, causes the

CARE OF LIGHTING SYSTEM (1949 ON)

Lucas-type dynamo to charge (see page 116) in all three lighting switch positions, which are as follows—

"Off" All lamps off.
"L" Headlamp (pilot bulb), and rear lamp, on.
"H" Headlamp (main bulb), and rear lamp, on.

On the coil-ignition models (65, 65 de Luxe), an ignition key is provided in the centre of the lighting switch, but this is quite independent of the lighting system dealt with in this chapter.

FIG. 64. THE LUCAS TYPE MCH55 HEADLAMP WITH BUILT-IN SPEEDOMETER, AMMETER, AND LIGHTING SWITCH

Fitted to all 1955-8 coil and 1955 magneto-ignition models. Fig. 66 shows the headlamp with the front removed. The 1956-8 MCH58 headlamp (fitted to Model 75) is similar

Is Lucas Headlamp Alined Correctly? Incorrect headlamp alinement and/or an out-of-focus main bulb give reduced road illumination and are liable to dazzle other road users. Both faults are simply rectified.

To check the headlamp alinement, take your Panther to a straight, level stretch of road, turn the lighting switch to the "H" position, and operate the dimming switch so that the main driving light is switched on. The beam of light should, if alinement is correct, be straight ahead and slightly below the horizontal. If the headlamp is mounted so that the beam of light is elevated or projects too much on the road, slacken the two side fixing-screws which secure the headlamp to its brackets and then tilt the headlamp slightly down or up until correct alinement is obtained. Afterwards tighten the two lamp fixing-screws firmly.

Is Headlamp Focus Correct? On 1949-54 Panther machines the double-filament main bulb is carefully focused to give the best illumination. Provided that genuine Lucas bulbs of the correct wattage and number are fitted as replacements, subsequent refocusing should not be necessary. Where a Lucas bulb is not available, or the focusing adjustment has been disturbed, it is necessary to re-focus. At the same time it is desirable to check the headlamp alinement as previously described.

The headlamp is correctly focused when the reflected rays of light are almost parallel and when the beam, projected upon a wall some distance from the machine, illuminates brightly a circular area of minimum diameter. The filament for the main driving light should be as near as possible to the focal point of the reflector in order to obtain a parallel beam. If the filament is positioned in front of the focal point, a converging beam (with dark centre portion) results. If, on the other hand, the filament is positioned behind the focal point, a diverging beam is obtained.

Both converging and diverging beams are highly undesirable as they illuminate the road poorly and are liable to dazzle other road users. Adjust the focus of the headlamp immediately if its beam is not uniform, is of short range, and has a dark centre. In order to focus the headlamp it is obviously necessary to move the main bulb backwards or forwards on the reflector axis according to whether the beam is converging or diverging respectively.

Focusing Lucas MU42 Headlamp (1949 to 1954). Take your Panther to a level stretch of road and focus the headlamp against a wall some distance (say 30-40 feet) from the machine. The lamp front and reflector should then be removed. Release the spring fixing catch provided at the bottom of the lamp (see Fig. 65) and withdraw the lamp front. Next withdraw the rubber bead and take out the reflector, complete with bulb holder which has a clamping clip for focusing.

To focus the main bulb, loosen the clamping screw on the clip and push the bulb holder in or out of the clamping clip as required. It may be found necessary to make several focusing adjustments. Having made each adjustment, replace the lamp front and reflector, and test the beam for correct focus as described in an earlier paragraph. On obtaining the correct focusing adjustment, retighten firmly the screw on the bulb holder clamping clip.

When replacing the reflector, locate the thinner lip of the rubber bead between the reflector rim and the edge of the lamp body. To replace the lamp front, locate the metal tongue in the slot at the

CARE OF LIGHTING SYSTEM (1949 ON)

top of the lamp, press the lamp front on, and then secure by means of the spring fixing catch.

Renewing Lucas Bulbs (1949 to 1954). When bulb renewal is necessary, always replace the old bulbs by new ones of *Lucas* manufacture, and of the correct type. The majority of large garages and accessory firms (see page 83) stock genuine Lucas bulbs, which are all carefully tested to check that the filament *is* correctly positioned to give the best results with Lucas reflectors. Do not wait until a bulb actually burns out, but renew it after

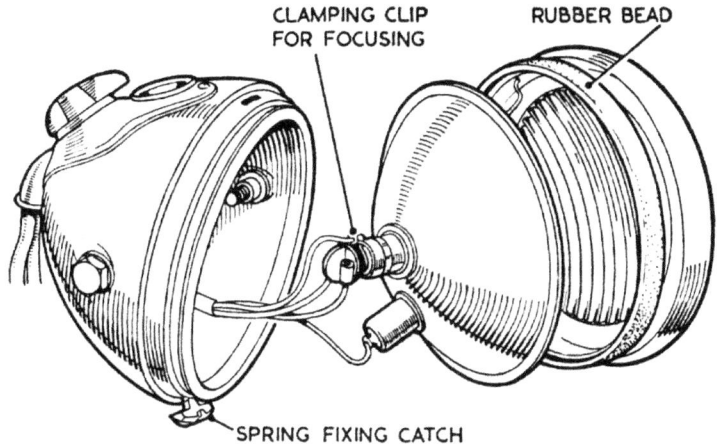

FIG. 65. LUCAS TYPE MU42 HEADLAMP WITH LAMP FRONT AND REFLECTOR REMOVED (1949-54)

Note the focusing adjustment on the bulb holder at the back of the reflector

long service. By doing this, the risk of incorrect focus being caused by a sagging filament is avoided.

The metal caps of Lucas bulbs are marked with a number for the purpose of identification. When renewing a bulb always verify that its cap is marked with the correct number. On magneto-ignition models (Model 75), the correct bulb number for the double-filament main bulb is No. 168 (6 V., 24/24 W.). For the headlamp pilot, and rear lamp bulbs fit a No. 200 (6 V., 3 W.) and a No. 205 (6 V., 6 W.) bulb respectively. For coil-ignition models (Models 65, 65 de Luxe), a No. 200 bulb is suitable for the pilot light and rear lamp, but fit a No. 168 main bulb (6 V., 24/24 W.) in the Lucas MU42 headlamp.

To remove a Lucas bulb from its holder, it is only necessary to release its bayonet fixing and withdraw the bulb. When fitting a double-filament main bulb, see that it is fitted the correct way round, i.e. with the dipped beam filament *above* the centre filament.

To indicate the correct position in the bulb holder the word "Top" is etched on each main bulb. After renewing a headlamp main bulb it is generally advisable to check the focus (see page 122).

The Lucas MCH55, MCH58 Headlamps (1955 On). No focusing adjustment is provided on Lucas-type headlamps fitted to all 1955 and later 250 c.c. and 350 c.c. Panthers. Each headlamp has a

FIG. 66. THE LUCAS TYPE MCH55 HEADLAMP WITH FRONT REMOVED (1955–8 COIL-IGNITION MODELS)
This headlamp applies also to the 1955 350 c.c. Model 75, but a Lucas MCH58 headlamp (similar, but larger) is fitted to all 1956–8 350 c.c. models
(*By courtesy of "The Motor Cycle," London*)

1. Ammeter
2. Speedometer drive
3. Speedometer
4. Speedometer bulb holder
5. Lighting switch
6. Main bulb leads
7. Tongue on lamp rim
8. Back shell on main-bulb holder
9. Reflector
10. Pilot-bulb holder
11. Spring-loaded catch
12. Ammeter leads
13. Ammeter-bulb lead

flanged "pre-focus" double-filament main bulb giving permanent focusing, and the pilot bulb is conveniently positioned in a holder (a push fit in the reflector) beneath the main bulb as shown in Fig. 66. An attractive feature of the MCH55 and MCH58 headlamps is the very neat installation of the lighting switch, ammeter, and speedometer (see Fig. 64).

To renew the "pre-focus" main bulb, remove the lamp front. Do this (MCH55) by releasing the spring-loaded catch (11) at the base of the headlamp and lifting the metal tongue (7) on the top of the rim out of the slot in the body of the headlamp. On the MCH58 headlamp (Model 75) loosen the screw on top of the lamp

CARE OF LIGHTING SYSTEM (1949 ON)

and pull off the lamp front and light-unit assembly. Turn the back shell (8) *anti-clockwise* on its bayonet fixing, pull it off, and withdraw the main bulb from the rear of the reflector (9). Then fit the correct bulb (see next paragraph) in the holder. The bulb slides down freely, and a projection on its flange engages a groove in the holder; it is thus quite impossible to fit the bulb incorrectly. Now engage the projections on the inside of the back shell with the slots in the bulb holder, press on, and secure by turning the back shell *clockwise*. Finally press the lamp front on, and secure by means of the spring-loaded catch (MCH55) or screw (MCH58).

Renewing Lucas Bulbs (1955 On). Note the remarks on page 123, concerning bulb filaments. See that each renewal bulb has the correct Lucas identification number marked on its cap. On 250 c.c. and 350 c.c. Panthers the correct bulbs required for renewal are as follows—

    Main bulb: 6 V., 30/24 W., double-filament, Lucas No. 312.
    Pilot bulb: 6 V., 3 W., M.C.C., Lucas No. 988.
    Speedometer bulb: 2·5 V., 0·3 amp., Osram.
    Ammeter: no illumination provided.
    Stop-tail lamp bulb (250 c.c. Model 65): 6 V., 3/18 W., Lucas No. 384.
    Stop-tail lamp bulb (Model 75): 6 V., 6/18 W., Lucas No. 384.

Cleaning Lamps. Clean ebony black surfaces with a good type of car polish. Chromium-plated surfaces do not tarnish and should be wiped over with a damp cloth occasionally in order to remove dirt or dust. Care must be taken when handling a reflector not to scratch it accidentally, and *on no account must metal polish be used to clean it.*

A fine colourless, and transparent covering is provided on all Lucas reflectors for protection purposes, and this covering can readily be cleaned without any risk of damaging the actual surface of the reflector. Polish the reflector covering lightly with a clean, dry, soft cloth or a chamois leather. No other treatment is desirable.

The Lucas Ammeter. This centre-zero instrument shows a charge on one side and a discharge on the other and is provided to give a reading of the amount of current flowing to or from the battery.

For instance, if the dynamo output is 3 amp. at a certain speed, and the pilot bulb and rear lamp are on, thereby absorbing, say, 1 amp., then 2 amp. remain for battery charging, and the ammeter will therefore indicate 2 amp.

At very low r.p.m. the ammeter reading is zero because the

dynamo armature is not rotating fast enough to generate sufficient current to give a battery charge. (See also page 116.)

The Ignition Warning Lamp. On coil-ignition models (65, 65 de Luxe), this is combined with the ammeter in the headlamp. It shows a *red* light when the engine is stationary with the ignition switched on, and it also lights up when the engine is idling. After a considerable mileage the bulb may "go west," and should be replaced by a Lucas bulb No. 998 (6 V., 0·1 amp.). To render the bulb accessible, detach the Lucas lamp front and reflector. Note that failure to replace the bulb does not affect the ignition system.

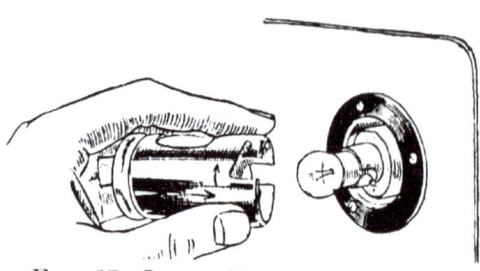

FIG. 67. LUCAS TYPE MT211 REAR LAMP (1949-54)
Fit the cover as indicated by the two arrows

The Lucas MT211 Rear Lamp. This rear lamp is secured to the rear number plate of 1949 to 1954 Panther models by means of a three-bolt fixing. To remove the cover carrying the red glass, push in and turn in an *anti-clockwise* direction. To replace the cover (see Fig. 67), locate the slots in the front portion over the retaining pegs in the lamp body, push inwards, and turn *anti-clockwise*.

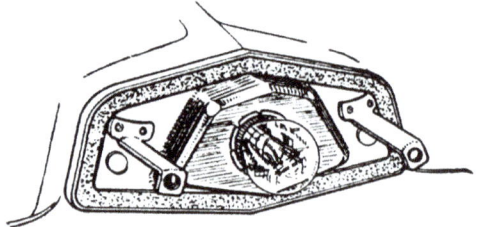

FIG. 68. LUCAS TYPE 525 STOP-TAIL LAMP
Fitted to 1955 and later Panthers

The Lucas 525 Stop-tail Lamp. This lamp is fitted to 1955-8 Panthers, and Fig. 68 shows the lamp with the red plastic cover removed. The bulb itself has offset pins to ensure correct fitting. The 3 W., filament (or 6 W., Model 75) provides the normal rear light, and depressing the rear brake pedal illuminates the 18 W. filament.

THE LUCAS HORN (1949 ON)

No adjustment or attention should normally be necessary, as the horn is carefully tested before being fitted to your Panther. Should the performance of the electric horn deteriorate and give a horrible choking sound, do not jump to the conclusion that a fault necessarily lies in the horn itself. It is far more likely that some other trouble is affecting the horn. For instance, the battery may be in a low state of charge (see page 120), a connexion may be loose, or there may be a short in the circuit.

Make quite sure that the horn push bracket is making good electrical contact with the handlebars. See also that the horn mounting is secure. Do not dismantle the horn if the trouble cannot be tracked down, but return it to a Lucas service depot for expert attention.

THE WIRING CIRCUIT (1949 ON)

Prior to removing the switch from the Lucas MU42, MCH55 or MCH58 headlamp or making any alterations to the wiring circuit, always *disconnect the positive lead at the battery*, so as to prevent the risk of a short-circuit.

The lead from the battery positive-terminal is connected by means of a brass connector to the lead from the lighting switch. A rubber shield insulates the connector and the former must be pushed back to enable the connector to be unscrewed. Be very careful not to permit the connector to contact any metal part of the frame, otherwise a "fat" spark will indicate that the battery has been well and truly shorted. Push the rubber shield right over the connector as soon as a connexion has been made.

Coloured sleevings as indicated in Figs. 69 to 73 identify the ends of all cables in the wiring circuit. To make a connexion to the switch (1949-54), remove the headlamp panel (secured by three screws). Then bare approximately $\frac{3}{8}$ in. of the cable to be connected, twist the wire strands together, and turn back about $\frac{1}{8}$ in. so as to form a small ball. Remove the grub-screw from the appropriate terminal and insert the wire so that the ball fits in the terminal post. Afterwards fit and tighten the grub-screw so as to compress the wire ball and thereby obtain a good connexion.

To make a connexion to the compensated voltage control unit or dynamo terminals, loosen the fixing screw on the terminal block and withdraw the clamping plate. Remove the metal sleeves from each terminal, pass about 1 in. of the cable through the holes in the clamping plate, and bare the ends for $\frac{3}{8}$ in. Fit the metal sleeves over the cables, bend back the wire over the sleeves, and push them right home into the respective terminals. After doing this, screw down the clamping plate firmly.

A Point to Note. Do not reverse the leads connected to the "D" and "F" terminals (see Fig. 61) of the C.V.C. unit or dynamo. To prevent accidental reversal, the screw in the dynamo terminal block is off-centre, and the screws securing the regulator terminal clamping plate are of different dimensions.

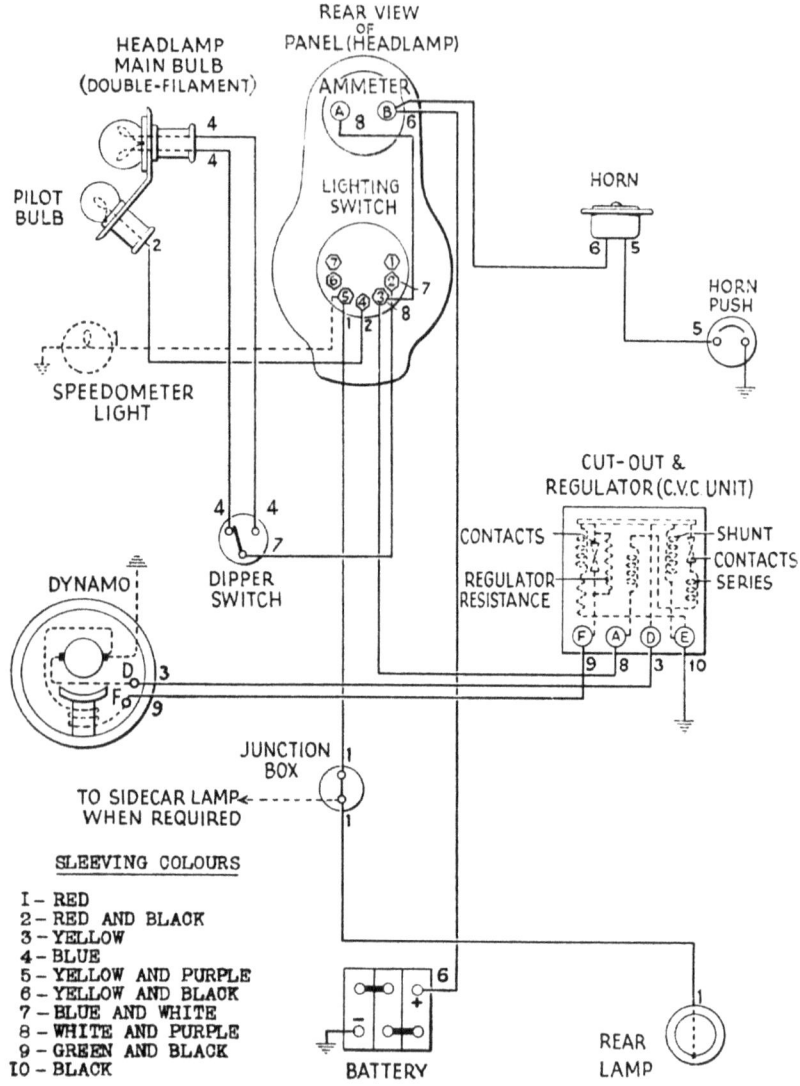

Fig. 69. Wiring Diagram for Lucas Dynamo Lighting Equipment (with C.V.C.) Fitted to 1949–51 Magneto-ignition Panthers

This diagram applies to the 350 c.c. Model 75. All internal connexions are shown dotted. On lightweight Panthers the junction box shown (for a sidecar) is not included in the wiring harness. The battery negative terminal is earthed

(*Joseph Lucas, Ltd.*)

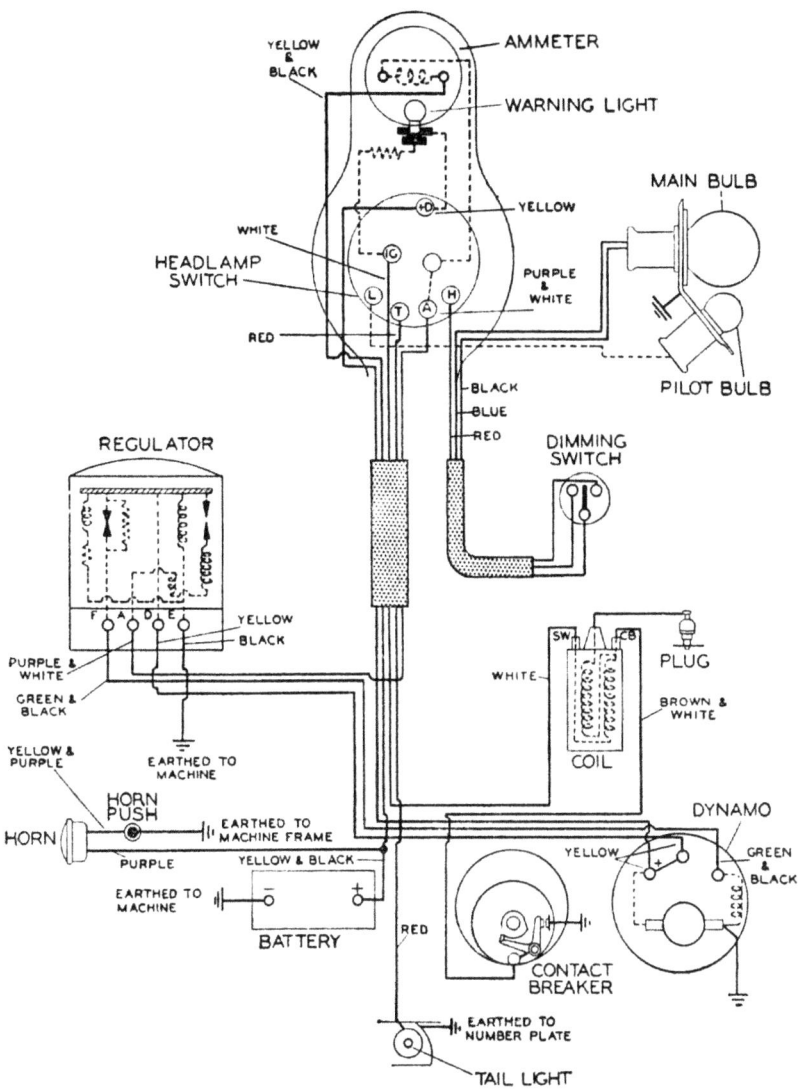

Fig. 70. Wiring Diagram for Lucas Dynamo Lighting Equipment (with C.V.C.) Fitted to 1949-51 Coil-ignition Panthers

This diagram applies to the 250 c.c. Models 65 and 65 de Luxe. All internal connexions are shown dotted. The battery negative terminal is earthed

(*Joseph Lucas, Ltd.*)

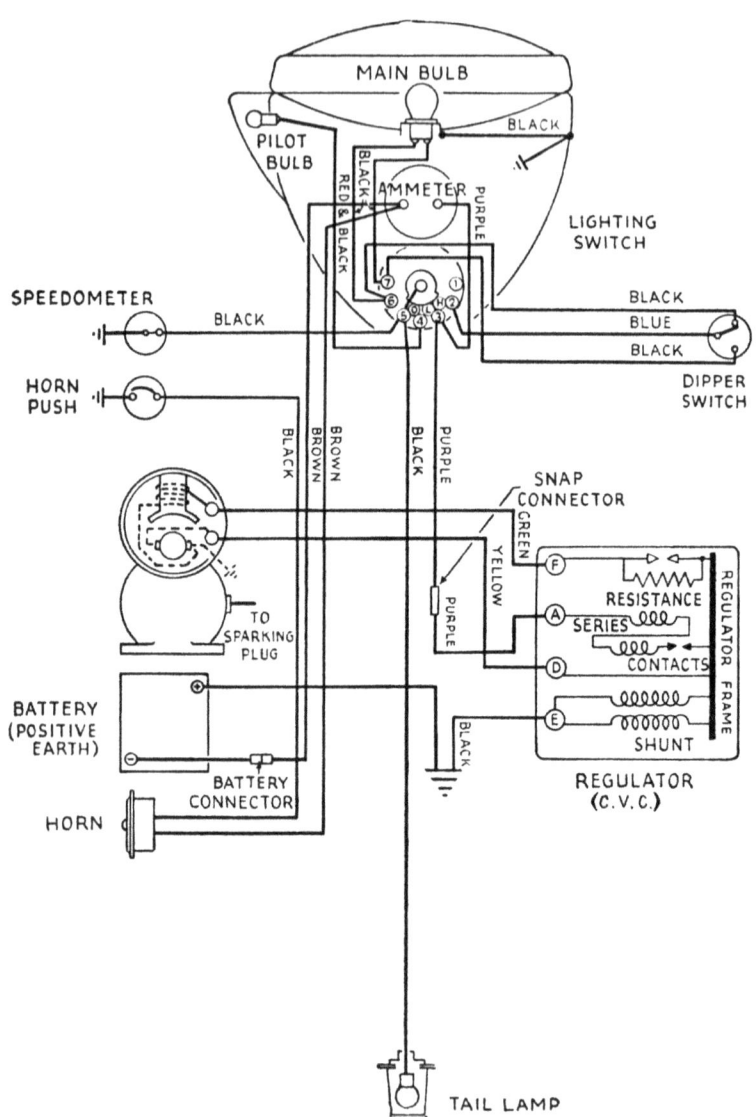

Fig. 71. Wiring Diagram for Lucas Dynamo Lighting Equipment (with C.V.C.) Fitted to 1952-4 Magneto-ignition Panthers

This diagram applies to the 350 c.c. Model 75. Note that the battery positive terminal is earthed. For 1955 a double-filament stop-tail lamp is fitted (wiring as in Fig. 73) instead of the tail lamp shown

(*Joseph Lucas, Ltd.*)

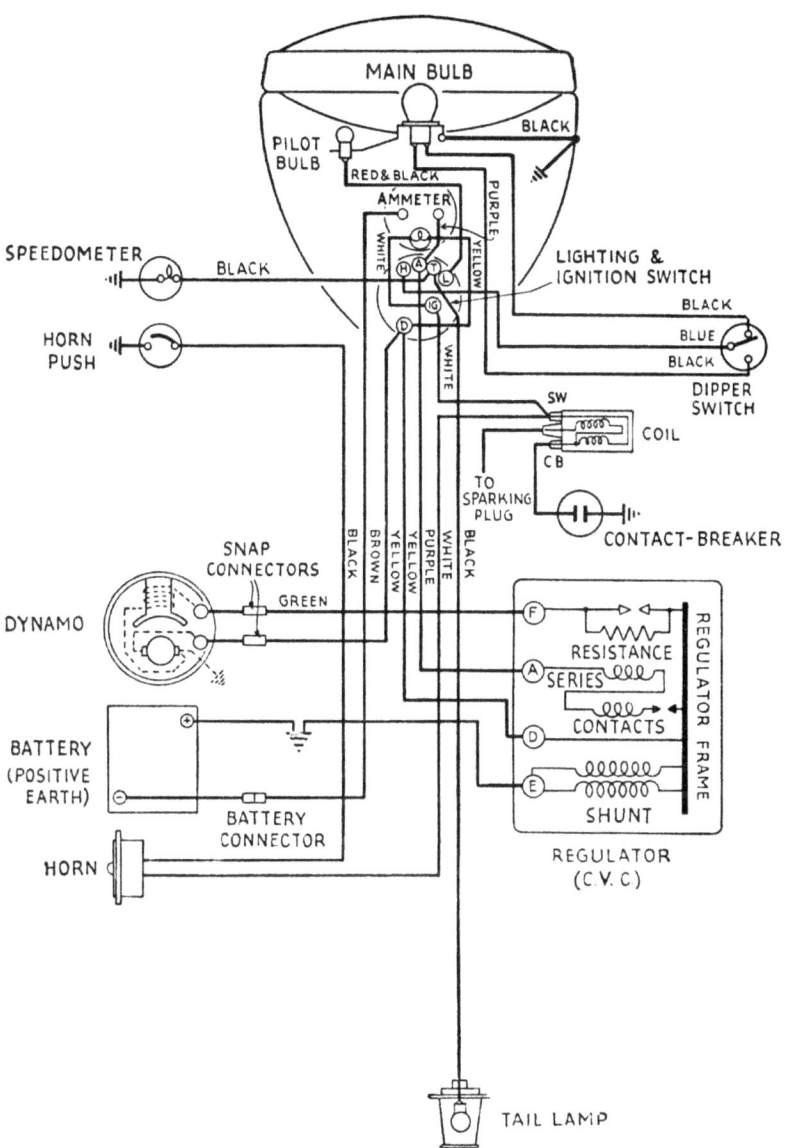

FIG. 72. WIRING DIAGRAM FOR LUCAS DYNAMO LIGHTING EQUIPMENT (WITH C.V.C). FITTED TO 1952-4 COIL-IGNITION PANTHERS

This diagram applies to the 250 c.c. Model 65. Note the earthing of the battery positive terminal. A double filament stop-tail lamp is fitted for 1955 instead of the tail lamp shown

(*Joseph Lucas, Ltd.*)

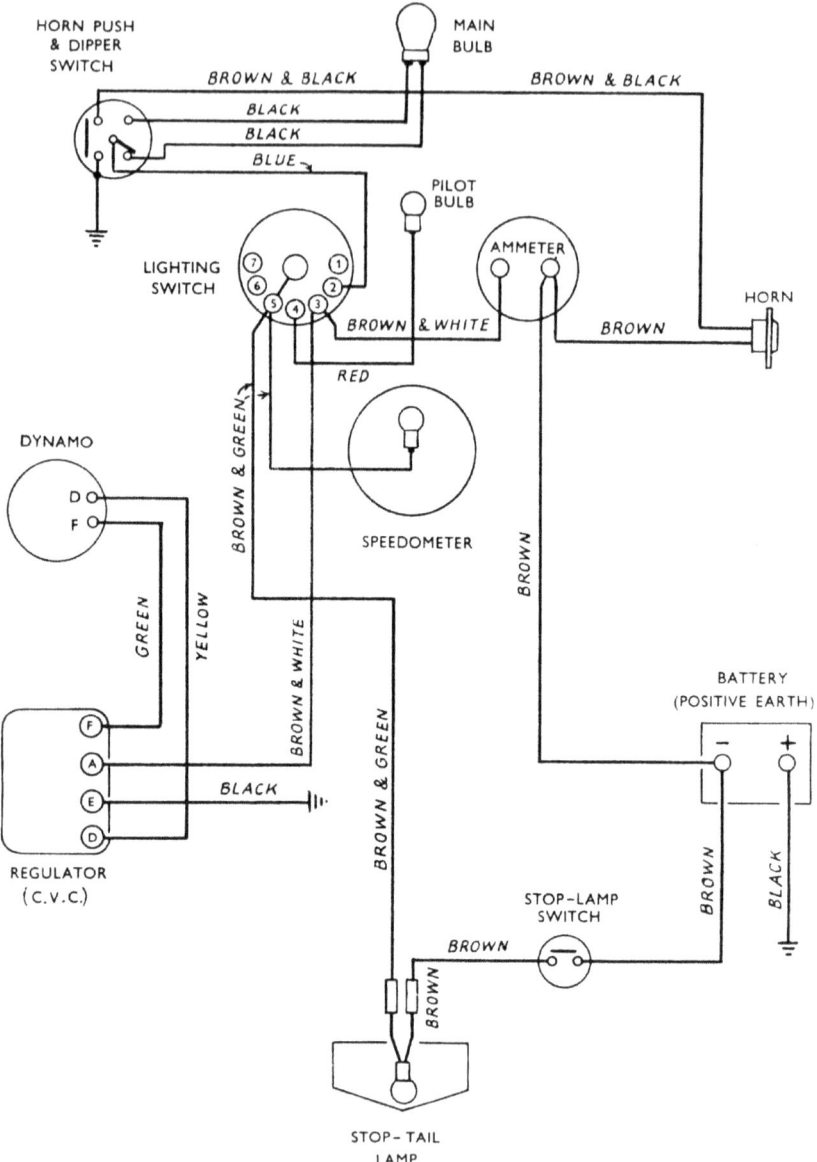

Fig. 73. Wiring Diagram for Lucas Dynamo Lighting Equipment (with C.V.C.) Fitted to 1956–8 Magneto-Ignition Panthers

This diagram applies to the 350 c.c. Model 75. The battery positive terminal is earthed, and the horn push and dipper switch are combined. Note that where two cable colours exist, the first indicates the main colour, and the second the tracer colour

(*Joseph Lucas, Ltd.*)

INDEX

Air-filter, 23
—— -release valve, 31, 34, 73
Alinement, wheel, 54
Amal carburettor, maintenance, 19
—— ——, tuning, 17
Ammeter, 8, 125
Armstrong unit, 105
Automatic ignition advance, 88

Battery, care of, 110, 117
—— "flat," 113
—— removal, 110, 118
Bearings, wheel, 54
Brakes, 56, 92
Brushes, commutator, 106, 115
Bulb renewal, 109, 123
Burman clutch adjustment, 51, 89
—— gearbox, 35, 76

Carbon deposits, 57, 62
Carburettor control adjustment, 57
——, assembling, 21, 23
—— maintenance, 19
—— settings, 17
——, tuning, 17
Chain case lubrication, 36
—— lubrication, 36
—— tension, 53-4, 89-91
Charging battery, 110, 116
Cleaning carburettor, 20
—— sparking plugs, 48, 73
Clutch adjustment, 51, 52, 89
—— drag, 75
—— plates, freeing, 6
—— slip, 75
—— springs, 75
—— sprocket, loose, 75
Coil maintenance, 88, 113
Commutator maintenance, 106, 115
Compensated voltage control, 112, 116, 127
Complete overhaul, 68
Comprehensive insurance, 10
Condenser, testing, 49
Contact-breaker, 49, 50, 84-7
Controls, 1, 57

Correct lubrication, 24-40
Cut-away, throttle, 14, 21
Cut-out, 106
Cylinder barrel, fitting, 66, 97
—— —— removal, 60, 94
—— head, fitting, 67, 97
—— —— removal, 59, 94

Decarbonizing, 57, 93
Dynamo failing to charge, 113
—— lubrication, 31, 35
—— maintenance, 106, 114

Engine lubrication, 24-35
—— oils, suitable, 28
Exhaust, colour of, 16
—— valve lifter, 4
—— —— —— adjustment, 47
—— —— ——, disconnecting, 73, 93

Filter, sump, cleaning, 30, 33
Finning, cylinder, cleaning, 66
Focusing headlamp, 109, 122
Foot control, use of, 7
Front forks, girder, 36, 56
——, telescopic, 37, 40, 77, 102
—— wheel, removing, 55, 91

Gear changing, 6
—— control adjustment, 52
Gearbox lubrication, 35
——, overhauling, 76
Gears, difficulty in engaging, 76
Gears jumping out, 76
Greases, suitable, 37
Grinding-in valves, 64, 95
Gudgeon-pin, removing, 60, 94

Handlebars, adjusting, 56, 82
Headlamp switch, 8, 120
Headlamps, 8, 120
Horn, 126

Ignition lever, 3
——, retiming, 71, 99
Inflation, tyre, 0

133

JET sizes, Amal, 17

KICK-STARTER troubles, 77

LAMPS, care of, 109, 120-26
Lubricants, chain, 37
Lubrication, motor-cycle parts, 35-40
——, dynamo, 31, 35
——, engine, 24-35
——, magneto, 34

"MAGLITA" contact-breaker, 50
—— lubrication, 31
Miller contact-breaker, 48
—— dynamo, 106
"Monobloc" carburettor, 16

NEEDLE jet, 22

OIL-BATH chain case, 36
Oil circulation, checking, 27, 29, 33, 67
—— level, engine, 28
—— supply to engine, regulating, 27
"Oleomatic" forks, 37, 77-81, 91

PANTHER lubrication, 24, 31
——, rear suspension unit, 38, 105
Petrol tank removal, 58, 93
Pilot jet, 18, 21
Piston clearances, 73, 94
——, fitting, 66, 97
—— removal, 60, 94
—— rings, removing, 60-62
Polarity, reversed, 106
Ports, valve, testing, 65
"Pre-focus headlamp, 123
Primary chain, tensioning, 53, 89
Push-rods, fitting, 67, 97

REAR lamp, 126
—— wheel removal, 55
—— suspension, 38, 105
Reflectors, cleaning, 125
Repairs, 83
Rocker-box, fitting, 67, 97
—— lubrication, 30, 32
—— removal, 58-9, 94
Running-in, 9

SECONDARY chain lubrication, 36
—— ——, tensioning, 54, 90, 97
Semi-wet sump system, 26, 31
Shock-absorber, transmission, 52, 75, 89
Shorts, preventing, 106, 114
Slip-ring, 87
Slow-running, 19
Spares and repairs, 83
Sparking plug gap, 47, 83
—— plugs, cleaning, 48, 73
—— ——, suitable, 9, 83
Specific gravity, battery, 112, 119
Speedometer, 37
Spring-frame, 38, 105
Starting engine, 4
Steering damper, 3, 56
—— head, adjusting, 56, 93
—— —— lubrication, 37
Stop-tail lamp, 126
Stopping, 7
Sturmey-Archer clutch adjustment, 52
—— gearbox lubrication, 35
Sump filter, cleaning, 30, 33
"Swinging arm," 38, 105
Switch, headlamp, 8, 120
Switching off ignition, 8

TANK removal, 58, 93
—— replenishment, 1
Tappet adjustment, 46
Taxation, 10
Telescopic forks, 37, 40, 77, 102
Timing gear, removing and assembling, 70, 98
——, ignition, 71, 99
——, valve, 69-71, 98
Tool kits, 42, 43
Tools for garage, 41
Topping-up battery, 110, 118
—— forks, 37, 80, 102
Transmission shock-absorber, 52, 75, 89
Tuning Amal carburettor, 17
Tyre pressures, 9
—— repairs, 55, 101

VALVE clearances, 44-6
—— guide clearance, 65, 97
—— guide lubrication, 30
—— lifter, disconnecting, 73, 93

INDEX

Valve spring compressor, 62
—— springs, renewing, 65, 97
—— timing, 69-71, 98
Valves, assembling, 65, 97
——, removing, 65, 95
Vokes filter, 23
Voltage control, compensated, 112, 116, 127

WARMING up engine, 6

Warning lamp, 8, 109, 112, 113, 126
Weak mixture, 16
Weatherproof plugs, 83
Wheel alinement, 54
—— bearings, 54
—— hub lubrication, 38
—— removal, 55, 91
Wiring circuit, 127
—— diagrams, 107, 108, 111, 128-32

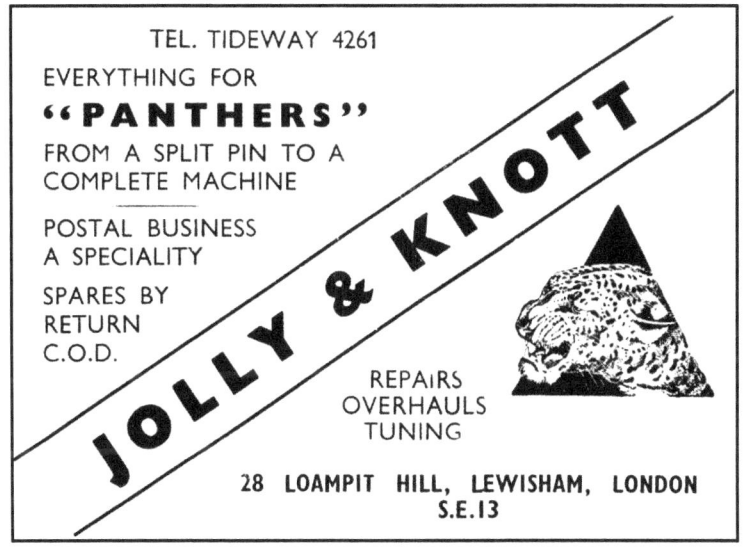

For a complete up-to-date list
and detailed descriptions
of all our titles, please visit our
website at:

www.VeloccPress.com

AUTOBOOKS WORKSHOP MANUALS

ALFA ROMEO GIULIA 1300, 1600, 1750, 2000 1962-1978 WSM
BMW 1600 1966-1973 WSM
BMW 2500, 2800, 3.0 & 3.3 1968-1977 WSM
BMW 316, 320, 320i 1975-1977 WSM
BMW 518, 520, 520i 1973-1981 WSM
FIAT 1100, 1100D, 1100R & 1200 1957-1969 WSM
FIAT 124 1966-1974 WSM
FIAT 124 SPORT 1966-1975 WSM
FIAT 125 & 125 SPECIAL 1967-1973 WSM
FIAT 125, 126L, 126 DV, 126/650 & 126/650 DV 1972-1982 WSM
FIAT 127 SALOON, SPECIAL & SPORT, 900, 1050 1971-1981 WSM
FIAT 128 1969-1982 WSM
FIAT 1300, 1500 1961-1967 WSM
FIAT 131 MIRAFIORI 1975-1982 WSM
FIAT 132 1972-1982 WSM
FIAT 500 1957-1973 WSM
FIAT 600, 600D & MULTIPLA 1955-1969 WSM
FIAT 850 1964-1972 WSM
JAGUAR MK 1, 2 1955-1969 WSM
JAGUAR S TYPE, 420 1963-1968 WSM
JAGUAR XK 120, 140, 150 MK 7, 8, 9 1948-1961 WSM
LAND ROVER 1, 2 1948-1961 WSM
MERCEDES-BENZ 190 1959-1968 WSM
MERCEDES-BENZ 220/8 1968-1972 WSM
MERCEDES-BENZ 220B 1959-1965 WSM
MERCEDES-BENZ 230 1963-1968 WSM
MERCEDES-BENZ 250 1968-1972 WSM
MERCEDES-BENZ 280 1968-1972 WSM
MINI 1959-1980 WSM
MORRIS MINOR 1952-1971 WSM
PEUGEOT 404 1960-1975 WSM
PORSCHE 911 1964-1973 WSM
PORSCHE 911 1970-1977 WSM
RENAULT 16 1965-1979 WSM
RENAULT 8, 10, 1100 1962-1971 WSM
ROVER 3500, 3500S 1968-1976 WSM
SUNBEAM RAPIER, ALPINE 1955-1965 WSM
TRIUMPH SPITFIRE, GT6, VITESSE 1962-1968 WSM
TRIUMPH TR4, TR4A 1961-1967 WSM
VOLKSWAGEN BEETLE 1968-1977 WSM

VELOCEPRESS AUTOMOBILE BOOKS & MANUALS

ABARTH BUYERS GUIDE
AUSTIN-HEALEY 6-CYLINDER WSM
AUSTIN-HEALEY SPRITE & MG MIDGET 1958-1971 WSM
BMW 600 LIMOUSINE FACTORY WSM
BMW 600 LIMOUSINE OWNERS HAND BOOK & SERVICE MANUAL
BMW 2000 & 2002 1966-1976 WSM
BMW ISETTA FACTORY WSM
CARRERA PANAMERICANA - MEXICAN ROAD RACE (BOOK OF)
COMPLETE CATALOG OF JAPANESE MOTOR VEHICLES
CORVAIR 1960-1969 OWNERS WORKSHOP MANUAL
CORVETTE V8 1955-1962 OWNERS WORKSHOP MANUAL
DIALED IN - THE JAN OPPERMAN STORY
FERRARI 250/GT SERVICE AND MAINTENANCE
FERRARI 308 SERIES BUYER'S AND OWNER'S GUIDE
FERRARI BERLINETTA LUSSO
FERRARI BROCHURES AND SALES LITERATURE 1946-1967
FERRARI BROCHURES AND SALES LITERATURE 1968-1989
FERRARI GUIDE TO PERFORMANCE
FERRARI OPP, MAINTENANCE & SERVICE H/BOOKS 1948-1963
FERRARI OWNER'S HANDBOOK
FERRARI SERIAL NUMBERS PART I - ODD NUMBERS TO 21399
FERRARI SERIAL NUMBERS PART II - EVEN NUMBERS TO 1050
FERRARI SPYDER CALIFORNIA
FERRARI TUNING TIPS & MAINTENANCE TECHNIQUES
HENRY'S FABULOUS MODEL "A" FORD
HOW TO BUILD A FIBERGLASS CAR
HOW TO BUILD A RACING CAR
HOW TO RESTORE THE MODEL 'A' FORD
IF HEMINGWAY HAD WRITTEN A RACING NOVEL
JAGUAR E-TYPE 3.8 & 4.2 WSM
LE MANS 24 (THE BOOK THAT THE FILM WAS BASED ON)
MASERATI BROCHURES AND SALES LITERATURE
MASERATI OWNER'S HANDBOOK
METROPOLITAN FACTORY WSM
MGA & MGB OWNERS HANDBOOK & WSM
MG MIDGET TC, TD, TF & TF1500 WORKSHOP MANUAL
OBERT'S FIAT GUIDE
PERFORMANCE TUNING THE SUNBEAM TIGER
PORSCHE 356 1948-1965 WSM
PORSCHE 912 WSM
SOUPING THE VOLKSWAGEN
SOLEX CARBURETORS (EMPHASIS ON UK & EU AUTOMOBILES)
SU CARBURETORS (EMPHASIS ON UK AUTOMOBILES)
TRIUMPH TR2, TR3, TR4 1953-1965 WSM
TUNING FOR SPEED (P.E. IRVING)
VEDA ORR'S NEW REVISED HOT ROD PICTORIAL
VOLKSWAGEN TRANSPORTER, TRUCKS, STATION WAGONS WSM
VOLVO 1944-1968 ALL MODELS WSM
WEBER CARBURETORS (EMPHASIS ON ALFA & FIAT)

VELOCEPRESS THREE WHEELER BOOKS & MANUALS

BSA THREE WHEELER (BOOK OF)

BROOKLANDS BOOKS & ROAD TEST PORTFOLIOS (RTP)

AC CARS 1904-2009
ALFA ROMEO 1920-1933 ROAD TEST PORTFOLIO
ALFA ROMEO 1934-1940 ROAD TEST PORTFOLIO
BRABHAM RALT HONDA THE RON TAURANAC STORY
BUGATTI TYPE 10 TO TYPE 40 ROAD TEST PORTFOLIO
BUGATTI TYPE 10 TO TYPE 251 ROAD TEST PORTFOLIO
BUGATTI TYPE 41 TO TYPE 55 ROAD TEST PORTFOLIO
BUGATTI TYPE 57 TO TYPE 251 ROAD TEST PORTFOLIO
DELAHAYE ROAD TEST PORTFOLIO
FERRARI ROAD CARS 1946-1956 ROAD TEST PORTFOLIO
FIAT 500 1936-1972 ROAD TEST PORTFOLIO
FIAT DINO ROAD TEST PORTFOLIO
HISPANO SUIZA ROAD TEST PORTFOLIO
HONDA ST1100/ST1300 PAN EUROPEAN 1990-2002 RTP
JAGUAR MK1 & MK2 ROAD TEST PORTFOLIO
LOTUS CORTINA ROAD TEST PORTFOLIO
MV AGUSTA F4 750 & 1000 1997-2007 ROAD TEST PORTFOLIO
TATRA CARS ROAD TEST PORTFOLIO

VELOCEPRESS MOTORCYCLE BOOKS & MANUALS

1930'S BRITISH MOTORCYCLE CARBS & ELEC COMPONENTS (BOOK OF)
1930'S BRITISH MOTORCYCLE GEARBOXES & CLUTCHES (BOOK OF)
AJS SINGLES & TWINS 250cc THRU 1000cc 1932-1948 (BOOK OF)
AJS SINGLES 1955-65 350cc & 500cc (BOOK OF)
AJS SINGLES 1945-60 350cc & 500cc MODELS 16 & 18 (BOOK OF)
ARIEL 1939-1960 4 STROKE SINGLES (BOOK OF)
ARIEL LEADER & ARROW 1958-1964 (BOOK OF)
ARIEL MOTORCYCLES 1933-1951 WSM
ARIEL PREWAR MODELS 1932-1939 (BOOK OF)
BMW M/CYCLES R26 R27 (1956-1967) FACTORY WSM
BMW M/CYCLES R50 R50S R60 R69S (1955-1969) FACTORY WSM
BSA BANTAM ALL MODELS FROM 1948 ONWARDS (BOOK OF)
BSA SINGLES & V-TWINS UP TO 1927 (BOOK OF)
BSA SINGLES & V-TWINS UP TO 1935 (BOOK OF)
BSA SINGLES & V-TWINS 1936-1939 (BOOK OF)
BSA SINGLES & V-TWINS 1936-1952 (BOOK OF)
BSA OHV & SV SINGLES 250-600cc 1945-1954 (BOOK OF)
BSA OHV & SV SINGLES - 250cc 1954-1970 (BOOK OF)
BSA OHV SINGLES 350 & 500cc 1955-1967 (BOOK OF)
BSA TWINS 1948-1962 (BOOK OF)
BSA TWINS 1962-1969 (SECOND BOOK OF)
CATALOG OF BRITISH MOTORCYCLES (1951 MODELS)
DOUGLAS PRE-WAR ALL MODELS 1929-1939 (BOOK OF)
DOUGLAS POST-WAR ALL MODELS 1948-1957 FACTORY WSM
DUCATI 160cc, 250cc & 350cc OHC MODELS FACTORY WSM
HONDA 50 ALL MODELS UP TO 1970 INC MONKEY & TRAIL (BOOK OF)
HONDA 90 ALL MODELS UP TO 1966 (BOOK OF)
HONDA MOTORCYCLES 125-150 TWINS C/CS/CB/CA WSM
HONDA MOTORCYCLES 250-305 TWINS C/CS/CB WSM
HONDA MOTORCYCLES C100 SUPER CUB WSM
HONDA MOTORCYCLES C110 SPORT CUB 1962-1969 WSM
HONDA TWINS & SINGLES 50cc THRU 305cc 1960-1966 (BOOK OF)
HONDA TWINS ALL MODELS 125cc THRU 450cc UP TO 1968 (BOOK OF)
INDIAN PONYBIKE, BOY RACER & PAPOOSE ILL PARTS LIST & SALES LIT
J.A.P. ENGINES 1927-1952 & MOTORCYCLES 1934-1952 (BOOK OF)
LAMBRETTA ALL 125 & 150cc MODELS 1947-1957 (BOOK OF)
LAMBRETTA LI & TV MODELS 1957-1970 (SECOND BOOK OF)
MATCHLESS 350 & 500cc SINGLES 1945-1956 (BOOK OF)
MATCHLESS 350 & 500cc SINGLES 1955-1966 (BOOK OF)
MOTORCYCLE ENGINEERING (P. E. Irving)
NORTON 1932-1947 (BOOK OF)
NORTON 1938-1956 (BOOK OF)
NORTON DOMINATOR TWINS 1955-1965 (BOOK OF)
NORTON MODELS 19, 50 & ES2 1955-1963 (BOOK OF)
NORTON MOTORCYCLES 1957-1970 FACTORY WSM
NORTON PREWAR MODELS 1932-1939 (BOOK OF)
NSU PRIMA ALL MODELS 1956-1964 (BOOK OF)
NSU QUICKLY ALL MODELS 1953-1963 (BOOK OF)
PANTHER LIGHTWEIGHT MOTORCYCLES 250 & 350cc (BOOK OF)
RALEIGH MOPEDS 1960-1969 (BOOK OF)
RALEIGH MOTORCYCLES 1919-1933 (BOOK OF)
ROYAL ENFIELD SINGLES & V TWINS 1934-1946 (BOOK OF)
ROYAL ENFIELD SINGLES & V TWINS 1937-1953 (BOOK OF)
ROYAL ENFIELD SINGLES 1946-1962 (BOOK OF)
ROYAL ENFIELD 736cc INTERCEPTOR FACTORY WSM
ROYAL ENFIELD 250cc & 350cc SINGLES 1958-1966 (SECOND BOOK OF)
RUDGE MOTORCYCLES 1933-1939 (BOOK OF)
SPEED AND HOW TO OBTAIN IT
SUNBEAM MOTORCYCLES 1928-1939 (BOOK OF)
SUNBEAM S7 & S8 1946-1957 (BOOK OF)
SUZUKI 50cc & 80cc UP TO 1966 (BOOK OF)
SUZUKI T10 1963-1967 FACTORY WSM
SUZUKI T20 & T200 1965-1969 FACTORY WSM
TRIUMPH PRE-WAR MOTORCYCLE 1935-1939 (BOOK OF)
TRIUMPH MOTORCYCLES 1935-1949 (BOOK OF)
TRIUMPH MOTORCYCLES 1937-1951 WSM
TRIUMPH MOTORCYCLES 1945-1955 FACTORY WSM
TRIUMPH TWINS 1945-1958 (BOOK OF)
TRIUMPH TWINS 1956-1969 (BOOK OF)
VELOCETTE ALL SINGLES & TWINS 1925-1970 (BOOK OF)
VESPA 1951-1961 (BOOK OF)
VESPA 125 & 150cc & GS MODELS 1955-1963 (SECOND BOOK OF)
VESPA 90, 125 & 150cc 1963-1972 (THIRD BOOK OF)
VESPA GS & SS 1955-1968 (BOOK OF)
VILLIERS ENGINE UP TO 1959 INC. 3 WHEELERS (BOOK OF)
VILLIERS ENGINE UP TO 1969 (BOOK OF)
VINCENT MOTORCYCLES 1935-1955 WSM

www.ingramcontent.com/pod-product-compliance
Lightning Source LLC
Chambersburg PA
CBHW070552170426
43201CB00012B/1819